T0270307

COLD WAR 2.0

Celebrating 35 Years of
Penguin Random House India

COLD WAR 2.0

Illusion versus Reality

MADHAV DAS NALAPAT

PENGUIN
VIKING
An imprint of Penguin Random House

VIKING

USA | Canada | UK | Ireland | Australia
New Zealand | India | South Africa | China | Singapore

Viking is part of the Penguin Random House group of companies
whose addresses can be found at global.penguinrandomhouse.com

Published by Penguin Random House India Pvt. Ltd
4th Floor, Capital Tower 1, MG Road,
Gurugram 122 002, Haryana, India

Penguin
Random House
India

First published in Viking by Penguin Random House India 2023

Copyright © Madhav Das Nalapat 2023

All rights reserved

10 9 8 7 6 5 4 3 2 1

The views and opinions expressed in this book are the author's own and the
facts are as reported by him which have been verified to the extent possible,
and the publishers are not in any way liable for the same.

ISBN 9780670098415

Typeset in Minion Pro by Manipal Technologies Limited, Manipal
Printed at Thomson Press India Ltd, New Delhi

www.penguin.co.in

MIX
Paper from
responsible sources
FSC® C010615

Contents

Foreword
Shivshankar Menon

As we enter the new and dangerous decade of the twenties, it is natural that we, in India, are faced with a series of challenges to our understanding of the international situation and to the methods that we use to arrive at that understanding. In this book, Professor Madhav Nalapat has given us an Indian view of one of the central features of our times, major power rivalry, particularly that between China and the US, concentrating on how it affects India.

Among the central issues that he addresses are the nature of the international system, the central role of major power rivalry in the international system today, and whether the US and China are engaged in a Cold War 2.0. This work approaches these fundamental questions from a realist perspective, in terms of international relations (IR) theory, and argues that the US-China Cold War 2.0 is a defining feature of our time. Professor Nalapat examines the policies of China, the US, Russia, Japan, India and the European Union (EU) in considerable detail, and then considers the interplay between the powers and the various factors that he identifies as critical to their geopolitical policies. While alternative answers to the questions he poses are possible and have been expressed in India, the pressure of events, particularly Chinese behaviour on the India-China border since spring 2021, has led to many of Professor Nalapat's views rapidly becoming the mainstream of broad segments of Indian opinion.

The conclusions that this book draws for India's policies from its examination of the present situation around India and the geopolitical context is to argue for a more assertive Indian policy stance with a tighter bond with the US. It is argued here that non-alignment and the pursuit of 'Strategic Autonomy' are to blame for India lagging behind other Asian powers economically. While that can be debated, and will be for some time to come, his prescriptions, many of which begin at home with the education of the underprivileged, the maintenance of social and communal harmony, and for strengthening India internally, should evoke a wide consensus among Indians of all political inclinations.

We are fortunate in India to have a robust tradition of debate and argumentation on national issues that matter. It is a welcome development that that tradition is now being extended to the realm of foreign and security policy as well. Professor Nalapat's book represents a significant Indian point of view and is thus a useful and knowledgeable contribution to that Indian debate. For it is only through democratic debate and the clash of ideas that we will learn to see the world through our own eyes, and to pursue India's interests as a nation.

1

Policy as the Centre Point of Geopolitical Analysis

The reality and circumstances of the life of a people evolve faster than the academic studies of such processes. The difference between analysis and reality is a lag, that in much of the theory of geopolitics is often almost or even more than a century old. Alfred Thayer Mahan and Halford G. Mackinder are considered the founding thinkers of geopolitics. The former stressed the importance of sea power, and the latter the need for control over the 'heartland'. Their respective continents, Brazil and the United States, have about the same area of land, but the trajectories of the two have differed substantially. And control of sea lanes was less the cause than the consequence of the expansion of the British Empire. What counts in order to ensure success is the application of mind and willpower directed towards the formulation of policies and consequent actions that facilitate the objectives sought. Often, such a choice may mean seizing an opportunity rather than ignoring it. Rather than such thought and action being planned and carried out solely or even principally within the confines of the formal governance system of a state, broad involvement of civil society in such processes adds to their efficacy.

The importance of the study and practice of geopolitics vests in a clearer visualization of the pathways that are available to policymakers—paths that convert potential into reality. The term 'policymaker' ought not to refer just to those at the apex of the governmental machinery in a country, and in its subsidiary units of governance, but to every citizen who exhibits the capacity and the will to take individual decisions that could majorly affect what has conventionally been termed 'ground reality'. The greater the number of such individuals within a given population, and the higher the level of autonomy given to them under the prevailing governance system to pursue their goals, the more would be the opportunities discovered—be for conversion of concept into substance, or ideas into action and result.

Looking at the last three centuries, individual 'decision-making units' (DMU) had a much greater degree of autonomy in the United Kingdom and the United States than their counterparts in—for example—the Empire of the Tsars in Russia, or in Medieval Spain. Countries where governance structures followed the 'top-down' model had a much lower level of DMU autonomy than countries where citizens had far greater freedom of action. The economic success of the People's Republic of China (PRC) may be presented as a counter to such a view, in that an authoritarian governance structure delivered rates of economic growth unprecedented during the last three centuries. In actuality, much of China's economic successes owed their origins to the substantial degree of local and functional autonomy that were in effect enjoyed by party units even in villages or small towns. The mayor of a large city in China, such as Guangzhou or Shanghai, has more powers (or had, now that Xi Jinping has begun curtailing DMU autonomy) than the chief minister of an Indian state.

During the 'Deng Xiaoping Model' period of China's rapid growth, which broadly continued until the advent of Xi Jinping in 2012, decision-making authority in economic matters got substantially devolved down the line.[1] Local and regional party functionaries had much more responsibility and autonomy in decision-making than has been the case in India until the present. Such lack of autonomy is the consequence of the central government's grasp on decision-making at almost all levels of authority in the world's most populous democracy. From 1981 onwards, until a comprehensive consolidation of powers by the Communist Party of China (CPC), also known as the Chinese Communist Party (CCP), General Secretary Xi Jinping during 2012–15, administrative powers were substantially devolved within the different layers of the party cadres in the PRC. It was not a coincidence that this period saw a sharp rise in the annual rate of growth of the country. This would not have been possible without the devolution of authority witnessed since the 1980s.

Given the rejection from the second half of the twentieth century onwards of pseudo-scientific theories about 'greater' and 'lesser' races, added to the fact that every human being has the inner potential to achieve excellence in some field or another, it follows that land or sea assets need not mandatorily affect the geopolitical advancement of a country within the international order. Japan for a considerable period of time had more influence globally than its much bigger neighbour, China. As did the US throughout the twentieth century despite the much larger Russian land mass. The primacy of Britain as the global centre of gravity began to get eclipsed after the 1914–19 conflict between European powers, a war in which

---

[1] Mingxing Liu, Victor Shih and Dong Zhang, 'The Fall of the Old Guards: Explaining Decentralization in China', *Studies in Comparative International Development* 53, (December 2018), https://doi.org/10.1007/s12116-018-9267-0.

the US came on the side of Britain only late into the conflict. After World War I, it was becoming clearer that the sun was indeed setting on the British Empire, while rising on the Pax Americana. The primacy of London was comprehensively eclipsed by Washington during the 1939–45 World War ignited by Adolf Hitler soon after the uncontested union of Austria with Germany in 1938. In modern times, what is being witnessed since the consolidation of control of the CCP by General Secretary Xi Jinping is Beijing overtly seeking to replace Washington as the centre point of global geopolitical gravity. Unlike what took place between Britain and the US earlier in the previous century, in the twenty-first century, the PRC is facing determined resistance rather than acquiescence at its moves aimed at displacing the US.

The earlier Cold War (Cold War 1.0) was between the Union of Soviet Socialist Republics (USSR) and the US. Although it is still continuously denied by a shrinking number of analysts, the world is witnessing a new Cold War (Cold War 2.0) between the US and China.[2] As happened in the earlier clash of superpower interests, this too is on track to end in the discrediting if not the dismantling of either the US or the PRC system of governance, accompanied by tectonic changes in the leadership and in policies of the vanquished power. The difference between Cold War 1.0 and Cold War 2.0 is that this time around, a direct rather than a proxy conflict between the two superpowers in any of the flashpoints that are emerging appears more difficult to avoid than during Cold War 1.0.

Indeed, some regard such a kinetic outcome as inevitable, given that Xi Jinping does not respect 'Spheres of Influence'

---

[2] M.D. Nalapat, 'President Biden Will Pick Up the PRC's Gauntlet', *Sunday Guardian*, November 28, 2020, https://www.sundayguardianlive.com/opinion/president-biden-will-pick-prcs-gauntlet.

in Asia that in Europe from the 1950s onwards characterized the earlier USSR-US contest. There was a division between the Soviet Bloc and the others, and barring a few initial attempts to change loyalties in Greece and Italy, the USSR confined itself to this zone. In Asia by contrast, China under Xi Jinping is continuously expanding the Chinese 'Sphere of Influence', and in actuality, acting in a manner that suggests that the entire continent is within this sphere, with the primacy of the US being edged out everywhere.

After the bloodletting caused by Germany's 1941 attack on the USSR, after 1945, Moscow adopted a defensive strategy. Even when the USSR seemed to be on the offensive, as in its obsession to control countries in East Europe such as Hungary and Poland, the motive was in essence defensive. It was to create a land barrier to a feared attack by the US and its North Atlantic Treaty Organization (NATO) partners. After brief spells of experimenting with dalliances with Euro-communist parties in Italy and France, the Communist Party of the Soviet Union (CPSU) saw that such political parties had perceptions and ideologies that in major respects differed from the Moscow line. As a consequence, such parties were unwilling to act as the agents of the CPSU in the manner that almost all communist parties in Europe (and some in Asia) had done since the period when J.V. Stalin was in control of the USSR. This remained true in the Soviet Bloc until the advent of Mikhail Gorbachev in the 1980s. Whether it be in France or elsewhere in Nazi (NSDAP)-occupied Europe, much of the domestic fightback against German occupation and excesses was owed to communist 'partisans' sabotaging supply lines and harrying German forces to lessen the intensity of Hitler's war on them and the USSR.

Within Nazi Germany, communist cells played a key role in what little resistance there was within that country when Hitler was in charge. The role of communist parties in Nazi-occupied countries during World War II, after the USSR was invaded by Germany in 1941, has been underplayed in Atlanticist histories of that period, especially in France, where it was almost entirely the communists rather than the 'Free French' who were active in the resistance against German occupation. That it was CPSU General Secretary Nikita Khrushchev rather than US President John F. Kennedy who blinked first in the 1962 Cuban Missile Crisis was no accident. It was CPSU policy after the loss of life during the 1941–45 Great Patriotic War to avoid a direct, kinetic superpower confrontation, including in theatres where more aggressive kinetic action by Moscow would have almost certainly succeeded. An example was the hastily abandoned effort during 1948–49 at a Soviet takeover of West Berlin from the control by the Atlantic Alliance.

Finally, Moscow under Stalin accepted the status quo established in 1945, in which most of the city came under the control of the Allies. Whatever chances existed for the avoidance of Cold War 1.0 disappeared with the 1948–49 Berlin land (but not air) blockade ordered by Stalin. From that time onwards, a sinister hue became the norm in Washington while judging almost every action of Moscow, thereby making a test of wills and capabilities inevitable in secondary theatres once Moscow began using the same lens in judging the actions of the US and its allies.

Those in the US who had favoured cooperation rather than confrontation with the USSR lost ground to the other school represented by experts such as American diplomat George Kennan, who (correctly) identified the ideology of the CPSU as being incompatible with that of the US, even while having an inflated view of the CPSU's willingness to go into a kinetic battle with the US. It could, however, be argued that given the confidence within the CPSU from the 1950s until the close of the 1960s in the supposed inevitability of the expansion of communism in Asia and elsewhere, Kennan's policy of containment was inevitable. In several countries, those parties and groups hostile to the US and its European allies were backed by Moscow. There did appear to be space for a genuine detente between the US and the USSR during a part of the 1970s, but this was eliminated when Soviet forces invaded Afghanistan in 1979.

Earlier, Stalin (who sought for much of the 1930s to come to an understanding with Chamberlain and Daladier to jointly combat the threat posed by Hitler) was unwilling to risk the possibility of an actual kinetic conflict with the US even in order to secure what he regarded as a desirable acquisition, full control over Berlin. The USSR, had it continued with the Berlin blockade, would have entailed heavy costs for the US, including as a consequence of the Berlin airlift, but less than a year after it was imposed, Stalin ordered the end of the land blockade. This was in the expectation that US President Harry S. Truman would let bygones be bygones and revert to President Franklin D. Roosevelt's policy of conciliation rather than continue with a tension-filled situation. Truman refused to follow that script and became a 'Cold Warrior' with zest. As it turned out in the Berlin blockade, neither did the Soviet Vozhd (leader) cause a long-term problem for the other side, nor did Stalin succeed in his initial objective of taking back Berlin. That lack of persistence by the USSR in securing control over Berlin gave impetus to the containment lobby within the US, and helped enable them to overpower those who favoured a policy of accommodation out of worry that the Cold War would contain the risk of kinetic Soviet retaliation.

By the 1960s, the USSR-US Cold War had become a global battle of systems, with either one or the other at risk of failure.

As it happened, it was the Soviet system that finally collapsed before 1992.

After his Berlin setback, Stalin decided on a policy of incremental progress vis-à-vis the US and its allies, associates and satellites. He sought to secure the influence of Moscow one country at a time, or one group within a country at a time. His successors built up a hugely expensive engine of kinetic war without any intention of ever landing in a situation where they would need to use it against the other superpower and its close allies. No NATO member was directly threatened by the USSR during the entire period of Cold War 1.0. While credit is given to NATO for deterring any aggressive action by the Kremlin, the reality was that it had been CPSU's settled policy since the 1950s to not spark a superpower conflict. Indeed, the line was to avoid such an outcome, even if it were to entail concessions.[3]

The thirteen-day Cuban Missile Crisis in 1962 was hailed within his country as a victory for Kennedy, who apparently had faced down a warmongering CPSU General Secretary Nikita Khrushchev. In reality, the Soviet leader had no intention of going to war over Cuba, and hence Kennedy succeeded simply by calling Khrushchev's bluff. The effort by the USSR to win over its bloc countries in Asia, Africa and South America made the US-USSR Cold War intractable, but the trajectory of the consequent arms race may have been different, had the defensive strategy of the CPSU been accurately factored into the policy matrix of the Atlantic Alliance. Fear, especially by the leadership of the USSR, of a first strike attack by the US and its allies, spurred the arms race between Washington and a

---

[3] Martin J. Sherwin, 'The Cuban Missile Crisis at 50: In Search of Historical Perspective', *Prologue* 44, no. 2 (2012), https://www.archives.gov/publications/prologue/2012/fall/cuban-missiles.html.

tremulous Moscow. This was as illusory a dread as was the US obsession that the USSR was poised on the tip of war (limited or otherwise) against the US and its treaty allies. While blame has been laid on US army officer Dwight Eisenhower's famed 'Military Industrial Complex' for the feverish race to build more and deadlier weapons against what was assumed to be an incurably aggressive Moscow, feverish development of offensive capabilities by one side led to a similar spurt in the other. That much of the weapons of mass destruction (WMD) created during that period by both the USSR and the US had their origins in fear rather than in the actual risk of aggression is testimony to the lack of understanding of the other side by each superpower during that period.

So ingrained in the CPSU leadership's catechism was the policy of conflict avoidance with the other superpower that throughout the Afghan War (1979–88), the territory of Pakistan (regarded by Moscow as a treaty ally of the US) was spared. As a consequence, the mujahideen finally prevailed over Soviet forces and their Afghan allies, thereby bringing Afghanistan further down the road to violence. Had Peshawar and some other locations within Pakistan been targeted by Soviet aircraft and missiles, it is impossible to believe that the US would have risked a direct kinetic conflict with the USSR by intervening militarily in defence of Pakistan against the USSR. Offensive rather than lack of action by the Soviet Union against Pakistan, the country that was essential for the mujahideen in the battle against the Soviet occupation, would have sharply lowered the (US-supplied) assistance given by Pakistan to the irregular forces battling the Soviet military in Afghanistan. This would have resulted in a far less humiliating closure to that conflict than what actually took place in 1988, a disaster that had severe consequences for the CPSU.

The concessions made by President Donald Trump to the
Taliban in 2020 and the pell-mell withdrawal from Afghanistan
under President Joe Biden in 2021 affected the global credibility
of the US as a credible military ally.[4] Yet what was much worse
was the domestic and external impact on the Soviet leadership
of the 1988 retreat of Soviet forces from Afghanistan and the
subsequent failure of Moscow to ensure sufficient stocks of
armaments and ancillary necessities so that the Najibullah
government in Kabul retained power rather than getting
defeated by the irregular groups that had been active in the
campaign against Soviet forces. A similar knock-down effect on
US prestige has been the consequence of the 2021 withdrawal
of US forces in Afghanistan, accompanied by the White House
kneecapping the Afghan military by abruptly depriving it of the
logistics and other support needed to hold the Taliban at bay.
Instead, soon after all US forces and logistical help disappeared
from Afghanistan, that country's armed forces dissolved
helplessly while a collection of radicals regained control of
Afghanistan two decades after ceding power in 2001 after the
9/11 terror attacks.

The USSR drained its energy and resources into building
up WMD and conventional stockpiles that it had no intention
of ever using against its principal foe or any of its perceived
allies, except if it were itself first attacked by NATO. This,
of course, was a proposition that within NATO was never a
realistic possibility. As emphatically as during the Khrushchev
period, the CPSU policy of avoiding any risk of a kinetic
conflict with the US and its treaty allies continued during the
years in office of CPSU General Secretary Leonid Brezhnev.

---

[4] M.D. Nalapat, 'After Kurds, Now Afghans Get Betrayed', *Sunday Guardian*,
February 29, 2020, https://www.sundayguardianlive.com/opinion/kurds-now-
afghans-get-betrayed.

The new leader sought detente since taking over in 1964, and the USSR avoided activity involving any attempted seizure or control of land and other assets that was within the US sphere of influence or had a formal partnership with Washington. NATO was a military combination that was tasked with defence against a pre-emptive military attack by the USSR, when such a move was regarded by the Soviet leadership as outside the purview of acceptable decisions. Small wonder that NATO has been such a failure in several of the situations that involve actual combat. NATO's initial successes in theatres such as Afghanistan, Iraq, Libya and Syria were soon overtaken by disaster. Even in Ukraine, 'saving' that country has meant only a deeper plunge into its abyss of loss of territory and soldiery against the Russian Federation. It is this unwillingness to risk a conflict with Russia that has prevented NATO from itself entering the conflict that has been ongoing between that country and Russia since 24 February 2022, no matter that in the process, Ukraine has been suffering extreme privation as a consequence of the hope that NATO will join its fight against the Russian Federation.

Just as Soviet war planning during Cold War 1.0 was defensive at its core, so was it within NATO too. This seems to have been either unknown or disregarded by the CPSU leadership, which persisted in the belief that the clash of ideologies could at any time develop into a military conflict initiated by the US. This was a mirror image of the US belief that the USSR was on the cusp of launching even a nuclear first strike on the US. Hence the unprecedented military build-up by each of the two superpowers. As for Washington, the Soviet build-up of capabilities that were seen as defensive in Moscow generated the certainty that the USSR was intent on securing in a kinetic manner an expansion of its influence and control

over entities regarded as vital to US security. Such a misreading
of Soviet intent resulted in the steady modernization of a US
defence capability that had possessed the capacity to destroy
human life on the globe several times over.

More than availability of sea or land space, what matters
in the determination of outcomes is not just the collection but
the interpretation of data from the other side, so that actions
and policies reflect ground realities rather than misperceptions.
A country indifferently endowed may prevail over another
that is much more abundant in its resources, as Germany did
against Tsarist Russia during World War I or Japan against
Kuomintang (KMT)-ruled China in the 1930s. Britain and
Japan have shown how limitations of geographic size need not
matter to attain geopolitical significance.

It may be argued that Japan is representative of a centralized
governance construct, and hence does not fit the postulate that a
devolution of authority promotes success. While centralization
may have been the case when looked at through the narrow
prism of legalist analysis (in which formal structures are all that
get considered), in actuality, the period when Japan burst on to
the global stage (towards the close of the nineteenth century)
saw a domestic situation where there were several points of
authority, whether these were feudal lords, army commanders
or large industrial conglomerates. Even in the case of Japanese
military campaigns against China, the leadership of its
Kwantung Army frequently demonstrated a mind of its own,
paying scant attention to commands from headquarters and
causing of *fait accompli* that were subsequently legitimized
by Army Headquarters in Tokyo. Japan's fateful decision
to attack Pearl Harbour was an example of a choice taken in
a context where those doubtful of success were silenced by a
determined few who believed that the foe would continue to

weaken and choke Japan if (in their telling) an 'inevitable and necessary' attack to be delayed. As it happens, Pearl Harbour only succeeded in drawing the US into the war being fought between the Axis (Nazi Germany, the Kingdom of Italy and Empire of Japan) and the Allies, to the delight of the UK Prime Minister Winston Churchill, who had been attempting that feat since the war started.

The Japanese invasion and occupation of large parts of China did not fit Tokyo's signature narrative of a fightback by Asians against European hegemony, while the 1941 attack on the US Navy opened a front outside East and Southeast Asia with the US, a country allied with the same nations that the Japanese were displacing from their Southeast Asian empires. At the same time, hostilities with the USSR were absent almost throughout World War II. In contrast to Japanese overreach in Pearl Harbour, the other extreme was the way in which the territory of Pakistan was spared by the USSR throughout the 1980s Afghan War. Such a hands-off strategy ignored the fact that the conflict could only be brought to a tolerable conclusion, were the Pakistan military to cease being a force multiplier for those battling Soviet forces in Afghanistan. The attack on Pearl Harbour by the Japanese Navy, as also the attack by Nazi Germany on the USSR, represented transparent examples of overreach by the Axis powers.[5] It is the impact of actions and policies that determine outcomes, which is why an application of the unsentimental logic of geopolitics is needed for success in the securing of outcomes by a country.

---

[5] Clifton B. Parker, 'Axis Powers Miscalculated after Early Advantages in World War II, Stanford Scholar Says', *Stanford News*, December 12, 2017, https://news. stanford.edu/2017/12/12/axis-powers-miscalculated-early-advantages-wwii-stanford-scholar-says/.

Thanks largely to expansion under the Tsars, the USSR had ample physical resources, but was eventually on the verge of defeat in European Russia during 1941–42. Such a disaster was caused by the initial failure of the CPSU leadership led by Stalin to understand the mind of the adversary, and to frame policy in accordance with that, rather than in a manner that reflected perceptions of the adversary by policymakers within the governance system of the USSR. When intelligence estimates fall prey to the preconceived perceptions of top policymakers, such that data gets censored, filtered and presented in a form that fits the existing hypotheses of those at the top, actions and policy may fail to have the impact on the ground situation that they were intended for.

The twentieth century presents a trove of examples that illustrate such a risk, an example being the fixation of Stalin almost until the actual attack by Germany in 1941 that the reports being shown to him of Wehrmacht (armed forces of Nazi Germany) preparations for invasion was disinformation designed to provoke the USSR into taking steps that could trigger a conflict with Germany. Stalin understood the trigger-happy disposition of Hitler and the latter's use of the military as the primary instrument of policy and sought through conciliation to keep his country out of harm's way until Britain and its indispensable partner, the US, exhausted themselves, and so did Germany, in their battle with each other for supremacy. Stalin was aware that it was Germany that represented the most significant long-term threat to the USSR once the war began and focused on dealing with that country rather than initiating hostilities against Japan. In turn, Tokyo avoided initiating hostilities on the Soviet front while it was dealing with the conquest and absorption of territories in East and Southeast Asia. Additionally, there was the largely naval and subsequent land front that was initiated by the US after Japan's decision to launch what was expected to be a crippling strike on US Navy capabilities and national willpower at Pearl Harbour. In much the same way, Hitler's air war on Britain in 1940–41 was designed to promote the cause of those who favoured a negotiated peace with Germany. Instead, the Battle of Britain strengthened Churchill and the others who were determined to fight on.

Neither Germany nor Japan took seriously the innate capacity of the production processes in the US to turn out war materiel on a scale never seen before in human history, and this proved their undoing. On the European front, it was the combination of US materiel and the fighting spirit of the Soviet soldiers that demolished the claim by Nazi Germany that it was the home of the Master Race, the 'Herrenvolk'. What assisted in the defeat of Germany was the effort most apparent by 1943 of Hitler to centralize military decisions within himself rather than leave them to commanders in the field, as had been done during the years of victory (1939–42).[6] Those on the ground usually decipher the ground situation better than those further away, especially if the latter are in a thrall to accept theories and concepts that no longer bear any relation to the flow of current events.

Appreciation of the present danger, and a willingness to consider conclusions that differ from preconceptions are often necessary ingredients for success. The problem for several countries is that preconceptions survive long after they need to be abandoned. An example is the view that was fashionable in Washington from the 1980s onwards,

---

[6] Oron James Hale, 'Adolf Hitler as Feldherr', *Virginia Quarterly Review* 24, no. 2 (1948): 1.

and which still exists in several quarters, that the PRC, led by the CPC, can through concessions and cajoling become 'more like us' (or more like the US). Or to regard the Chinese people as identical with the CPC.

The trajectory of Cold War 1.0 reveals a trail of incorrect assumptions about the other side, leading to responses that ignore the logic of circumstantial evidence. Given that the USSR-US Cold War was about competing systems and spheres of influence, this proved to be a costly error. What in turn handicapped the CPSU leadership was an absence of knowledge about US intentions separate from the prismatic information secured through agents located there, most of whom were careful to adhere to the line taken by the CPSU leadership as a consequence of its misperceptions of the enemy country. Such axioms consequently coloured the information given by lower levels so that they better matched flawed perceptions rather than reflect the evolving reality. Given the containment strategy followed during Cold War 1.0, contacts between the USSR and the US were limited. In the case of the PRC, a 'constrainment not containment' strategy (first enunciated by India's first professor of geopolitics two decades ago) is increasingly being followed by the US in the case of the PRC, especially after 2020.[7] This is designed to keep open a variety of contacts with the PRC but try and avoid interactions that would significantly increase Chinese military capability. The weak link in such reasoning is to miss the fact that the Chinese method of war is hybrid, embracing efforts at hobbling not just a rival military but economies, healthcare and even an absence of high-decibel political and social differences that could slide into violence.

---

[7] M.D. Nalapat, 'Constrain, Not Contain, China', UPI, June 6, 2003, https://www.upi.com/Defense-News/2003/06/06/Commentary-Constrain-not-contain-China/17771054942105/.

While the CPSU leadership had too little information on the US, the CCP (or, as Beijing favours, Communist Party of China) leadership has ensured information on the US on a scale that often misguides and confuses policymakers in Beijing. This is the consequence of the use by the PRC of a variety of sources, whether these be citizens (many of Han origin) within the target country, as well as students, journalists, entrepreneurs or academics. Given the large numbers within such population clusters, the flow of information from and about the US to the PRC and its state and party entities is copious, making not less but more problematic the framing of smart policy about the enemy country in the era of Cold War 2.0.

The PRC has a centralized state structure that ensures the primacy of the CPC Standing Committee led by the general secretary in decision-making. Since 2012, authority has moved upwards to the office of the general secretary. Past ruler, 'Paramount Leader' Deng Xiaoping was similar to Mao in having a flexible approach to circumstances and policy designed to meet the exigencies witnessed. When Jiang Zemin took charge as CPC general secretary in 1989, throughout his decade in office, he devolved responsibility substantially to his subordinates. While there were some matters which he reserved to himself, including relations with the US and some business matters, overall, the devolution of governance under Jiang was similar to that under Deng.

When Hu Jintao took charge as CPC general secretary in 2002, and especially after he assumed the office of chairman of the Central Military Commission (CMC) as well in 2004, the significant change he made was to do away with the effective authority of 'non-formal' elements that in the past had the patronage of General Secretary Jiang. Such individuals during that decade had authority over matters even in the absence of formal mandates from the party or the government. In a way resembling the earlier example of the bureaucracy-backing leadership of CPSU General Secretary Leonid Brezhnev, Hu ensured that authority was disseminated only across the formal chain of command, the elements in which were careful not to tread on the interests of those close to CPC General Secretary Hu or his favourites. Whether it be the 'Shanghai Group' around Jiang Zemin or those who had been the favourites of Deng Xiaoping, Hu Jintao seldom interfered with the Deng and Jiang favourites, who had positioned themselves atop different authority chains within the PRC governance system.

Unlike Mao, Deng and Jiang, Hu did not seek to create a dispersed group personally loyal to him but confined his backing to a few party members by reason of their past association and service not just with him but with previous leaders of the CPC and the governmental structure controlled by it. This accommodative policy towards the existing bureaucracy began to change since 2012, the year when Xi Jinping took over as general secretary of the CPC and simultaneously as chairman of the CMC. Partly due to worry about elements hostile to him seeking ascendancy within the Party, such as the efforts by Bo Xilai to upstage Xi, or the moves by Jiang and Hu loyalists to limit his power, Xi Jinping began to oversee a process of steady concentration of authority to the Office of the General Secretary i.e., to himself.

The CPC general secretary overshadowed the prime minister of the PRC in a manner unprecedented since Mao. Premier Li Keqiang functioned in a manner that reflected the lack of authority he had to frame policies and implement them, save those proposed by the Office of the General Secretary. Xi has not been known for lack of self-confidence, so this has meant that significant elements of foreign and domestic policy in the world's newest superpower reflect the personality and views of the present CPC general secretary. This is similar to the situation that prevailed under Chairman Mao Zedong, who ensured that his preferences were what drove policy in the PRC, abandoning during the latter part of the 1950s his earlier practice of seeking to develop a consensus among the party elders in matters where the formulation of important policies were concerned. As was the case under Mao, CPC policy in the era of Xi reflects the personality and preferences of the leader rather than the earlier practice of developing a consensus based on multiple points of view channelled through party office-holders at relevant levels.

During the period in office of Jiang Zemin (1989–2004), barring issues dealing with his favourites, the general secretary was tolerant of diverse views, as was Hu Jintao, provided that such suggestions were moved through Party channels. Since 2012, views that go contrary to the Xi Jinping thought are regarded in much the same way as they were regarded by Mao, as disloyalty that in more than a few cases was held to amount to treason. As a consequence, the band of policy options that pass through the filtration process to the Office of the General Secretary has narrowed considerably, as has been the level of consultations that have taken place in the process of formulation of such policies. The trend has increasingly been to try and understand the views and preferences of the general secretary on a particular matter, and to make only such recommendations as reflect those opinions. This has had an obvious impact on policy, which has become (in a reflection of the personality of the CPC general secretary) far more expansionary and aggressive than had been witnessed since the period when Mao annexed Tibet, Xinjiang, Manchuria and Inner Mongolia to the PRC.

To such a list needs to get added the tendency of PRC policymakers to regard events as a straight-line progression rather than as a series of meanderings and zigzags. The increase in aggression of the People's Liberation Army (PLA) that was demonstrated across the Ladakh frontier in 2020 had its origins in the 'Teach India a lesson' school favoured by the PLA. An example of such aggression is what took place at Galwan in Ladakh in 2020, where too the Indian Army showed the same spine that was witnessed in Doklam in Bhutan in 2017, when moves by the PLA to take control of this territory were challenged by the Indian Armed Forces. This took place once the PLA reached points on the Doklam plateau from where they could overrun and thereby snap the 'Chicken's Neck' between Sikkim and Bhutan, a bite of land that is vital to the security of the North-eastern states of the Union of India. In the middle of 2020, the PLA sought fresh incursions into territory that it had earlier agreed was part of India, a move that resulted in the Galwan clash. It was evident that the PLA's moves had been approved by the CMC, which is chaired by Xi Jinping.

While much of the scholarship holds that the 1962 conflict was initiated by Mao Zedong as a consequence of the forward policy of the Indian military, another explanation could simply be the desire to cut India and particularly Prime Minister Jawaharlal Nehru to size. Similarly, were Xi Jinping to initiate a full-blown war across the Sino-Indian border, the objective may be to show not just India but the whole of Asia just who is *numero uno* in that continent. And to signal to NATO and the other three countries in the Quadrilateral Security Dialogue, also known as the Quad, (Australia, US and Japan) that India would be of very limited value to them in any confrontation with China.

Policy in India, especially on China, seems subject to a time lag between fast moving events and responses. The assumption made by policymakers in Delhi had long been that India should abide by the 'straight line' (of continuing policy) adopted by the Manmohan Singh government between 2004 and 2014. Before the 2020 clash, aggression on the border did not interfere with other issues such as trade, in which India proved helpful to China. These also included meetings of international organizations apart from trade and commerce. There remained in place tacit acquiescence in Chinese transgressions without any significant effort at recovering the ground lost, beyond the spoken or written word.

During the period when Manmohan Singh was the prime minister, expansion of PRC control over Indian territory on the border took place in small slices. In 2020, the depth and scale of the PLA advance was unprecedented since 1962—tactics that reflected the intentions of the CMC chairperson. After the 2020 intrusions, there was pushback by the Indian Army rather than past acceptance of an altered status quo. Soon afterwards, in another departure from past 'straight line' precedent, the Modi government imposed a partial ban on select Chinese apps, such as the widely popular TikTok, thereby explicitly linking events on the border to commerce, two silos that had been kept apart till then.[8] In a surprise operation, the Kailash Heights in eastern Ladakh were taken by the Indian Army, although vacated on the conference table later for the reason that belief in the PRC's benign intentions remains strong in the Lutyens Zone, even when the facts point the other way. It may be mentioned that the heights occupied by the PLA close to the Kailash Heights continue to be occupied by them, despite the show of goodwill and benign intentions evident in India's vacating the Kailash Heights soon after their capture in a way that has been absent in the case of Siachen.

---

[8] M.D. Nalapat, 'PM Modi Strikes a Deadly Blow to China's Tech Ambitions', *Sunday Guardian*, July 4, 2020, https://www.sundayguardianlive.com/news/pm-modi-strikes-deadly-blow-chinas-tech-ambitions.

Although Donald J. Trump, the 45th President of the US, veered off the essentially quiescent course adopted towards the PRC by Reagan, Clinton, Bush and Obama, he was regarded within the higher levels of the CPC as an aberration from the rule of US acquiescence to Communist China's rise. Despite his flurry of actions against China since 2018, it had been calculated within the CPC that the 46th President of the US, Joe Biden, would revert to the line followed by Bill Clinton and Barack Obama, and talk tough while acting in a much softer manner. It was a surprise when Biden similarly veered off course in the manner of his predecessor. Authoritarian systems find it more difficult to deal with surprises that less 'orderly' but more flexible democratic governance mechanisms are able to manage. The fact that Biden initially refused to follow Clinton and Obama but adopted the tough line (and talk) of his predecessor, surprised the CPC Standing Committee, especially the general secretary.

In early 2022, the Russian military's move into Ukraine diverted the attention of the White House back to Moscow from Beijing. Of course, Xi continued with his own 'straight line' of policy, which was to double down on his expansionary and assertive tactics rather than back down when confronted with pushback. If Stalin's expansionism and assertiveness after the 1939–45 conflict between the Allies and the Axis made Cold War 1.0 inevitable, it is similar aspects of Xi Jinping's policies and actions that have been the causal factor in Cold War 2.0, this time between the PRC and the US. The moves by General Secretary Xi for his country to displace the US as the apex of global power have been many and transparent.[9] These include

---

[9] Hal Brands and Jake Sullivan, 'China Has Two Paths to Global Domination', *Foreign Policy*, May 22, 2020, https://foreignpolicy.com/2020/05/22/china-superpower-two-paths-global-domination-cold-war/.

the Belt & Road Initiative, the subtle effort to dethrone the US dollar from its role as the global reserve currency, to cause fault lines within the EU, NATO and even the US homeland and to outpace Washington as the global leader in technologies. No matter how persistent the efforts of the Atlanticist establishment within Washington to refocus on Russia rather than concentrate on China, ground realities in the new Cold War will ensure that even the deeply Atlanticist Joseph Robinette Biden Jr will perforce have to accept that the twenty-first century is the Indo–Pacific century, even as the twentieth was the Atlantic century. It is this theatre of operations that will decide the victor of Cold War 2.0.

2

People's Republic of China: Foe as Friend

Through a variety of stratagems, almost all of which would have been vetoed by Mahatma Gandhi, who was obsessive about means rather than ends, Mao Zedong emerged during the 1930s as the leader of the CPC and went on to establish the PRC in 1949. Unwilling to accept its overlordship even during the Stalin period, Mao regarded the CPSU as the main obstacle to his planned installation of the CPC as the head of an international anti-colonial alliance that would in time and under his leadership displace the European colonial powers in influence and power. Unhindered by either received doctrine or personal consideration for other players, despite his chafing at the CPC's subordinate status, Mao saw in CPSU General Secretary J.V. Stalin a leader as ruthless as himself. The USSR under Stalin was a country to be respected, and therefore humoured. Chairman Mao adopted a policy of outward agreement with the views (read dictates) of Stalin in order to ensure that Moscow regarded him as a reliable and stable leader so far as the USSR was concerned and begin backing him within the

CPC.[1] Such a stance ensured a flow of Soviet assistance to the CPC that was routed through Mao and his supporters. Chairman Mao initiated a similar charm offensive with the US under President Franklin Delano Roosevelt, playing on the sentimentalism about China and its people that had been generated in the past by legions of Christian missionaries seeking to harvest millions of souls for redemption during the days of the KMT republic. Mao cast himself to his US interlocutors in the role of an agrarian reformer, who was motivated in his actions solely by the injustices meted out to small landholders and the landless by feudal elements in rural China. The CPC was presented as being free of graft, which of course it was in comparison to the KMT, where graft was the rule and honesty by an official was punished for showing disloyalty to the imperative of feeding superiors through the proceeds of graft. Higher officials were upset with an honest KMT official at being denied their slice of the bribes waiting to be collected, but which were not. In particular, the rapacity of the family of Soong Mei-ling, the spouse of Generalissimo Chiang Kai-shek, made Mao's task of wooing US interlocutors much easier than would have been the case had the KMT run the country better. To the US (in contrast to the Soviets, to whom he posed as a loyal admirer of Stalin), Chairman Mao cast himself in the mould of a Chinese nationalist, who would not accept his country's subordination to any other power, not even the USSR. To Moscow, he was the leader who understood the importance of the USSR and was eager to help promote Stalin's aims.

---

[1] 'Conversation between the Soviet Union's Joseph Stalin and China's Mao Zedong, 1949', USC US-China Institute, https://china.usc.edu/conversation-between-soviet-unions-joseph-stalin-and-chinas-mao-zedong-1949.

That was all the Marxist theory Mao needed to demonstrate in order to ensure continued assistance from Stalin.

Mao Zedong was indeed a passionate nationalist, but his convictions were not based merely on territorial or even cultural characteristics. Rather, it was as an expression of confidence in his own Han people, who from the start of the chairman's sojourn in politics were seen by the CPC supremo as the people that were the natural leaders of the human race. Unlike the primitive racism of an Adolf Hitler or the ethno-based racism of Winston Churchill, to Mao, the Han were more than an ethnicity, they were a civilization. The Han were the raw material available to him to mould once he assumed power over China. The founding father of the PRC saw the Han in an expansionary rather than in an exclusivist way. There has been much lifting of eyebrows at the manner in which minority groups such as the Mongolians, Manchurians, Tibetans and Uyghurs are being placed into a Han educational and cultural straitjacket, in the process getting them to shed their distinct societal and lifestyle characteristics. From the period in office of Chairman Mao onwards, such an acculturation process has been seen by China's leaders as not an act of oppression but the promotion of 'backward' segments of the population into the higher-quality Han mainstream. The minority groups are being assimilated into the Han population, so that eventually the PRC will be almost totally 'Han'. This is a process much like the children of Indian men and Han Chinese women living in China, who have been 'Sinicized' as a consequence of the educational and societal regimen that is followed within the PRC. Once such assimilation takes place, such children are not regarded as separate or unequal, but as an integral part of the population group that is seen by the CPC as destined to reclaim the role of the Middle Kingdom for the PRC. This is unlike societies where the tenets of Hitlerism are followed in a diluted manner, so that those of 'mixed race' are seen as separate from the mainstream population of the country.

Such a cultural assimilation, indeed submergence, of the non-Han minority and its ubiquity is core to the ideology of the CPC since its inception in 1921, although only since the assumption of the general secretaryship by Xi Jinping has this objective been expressed openly. Xi has been seen by the outside world as a change from his immediate predecessors. In actuality, the change is only in emphasis, transparency and form, not in inner substance.

The Chinese as a civilization have long been proficient in adapting to external circumstances, an example being the use of western names by those of Han ethnicity who settle in North America or Europe. Only within the home or among each other are their actual Chinese names used. Such adoption of a foreign name is a much more common practice among the Han than among the Tibetans, the Uyghur and other 'minority' nationalities, including those of the latter who reside outside the PRC. In India as well, foreign names have been in common use. These include the widespread use of Arabic names among Muslims, or European names among Christians, while the practice of taking a foreign name within India or abroad is not common among the Hindu majority. In the case of China and its people, it is the majority Han that has taken up such a practice.

Mao as the CPC chairman constantly sought to ensure that Stalin and the Soviet leadership saw the party in hues that were welcome to them. All this while a different visage was simultaneously presented to the US, the other country that the pre-1945 CPC depended on for assistance in its battle against the Japanese and against the KMT. During the war with Japan,

Mao was clear that the final battle faced by the PLA inside the country would not be with the Japanese (now that they were confronting a superpower and may in future have to directly contend with the second, as Japan's ally Hitler already was) but with the KMT and its affiliated armed groups. To the US, Mao highlighted the anti-Japanese facets in his information docket, while to the Soviets, he showed both that visage as also his determination to ensure that China joins the Soviet bloc, something that could take place only if the CPC prevailed over the KMT in the civil war between the two. Given Mao's demonstration of feigned fealty, Soviet assistance flowed mostly to the CPC, while help given by the US went to both the CPC as well as to the KMT, to the latter's chagrin.

The concentration of effort by Mao Zedong was not just to create a 'New China' but a 'New Chinese Citizen'. These were to be men and women committed to the 'Middle Kingdom' objective of the CPC, which aimed to make the PRC the global centre of gravity, replacing the US. Such a shift is Xi's China Dream up close. The Great Proletarian Cultural Revolution (GPCR) was a move by Mao to remove those in the CPC who resisted his imperious ways. Another reason was to convert the societal chemistry of the Han people by removing their awe of seniority, thereby better training them to resort to harsh physical and direct methods against opponents when called upon to do so. The impact of the GPCR on the psyche of the young during the 1960s has not been as carefully studied as was its impact on the Party leadership and its effects on the formal governance structure of the PRC. Those who participated in the Cultural Revolution (the Red Guards) were encouraged to believe fanatically in the objectives presented to them, and to hesitate not at all in using whatever means were at hand to bring these about.

Add to this the effect of the one-child policy, which was implemented in the PRC from the 1970s. Single male children in particular were indulged by parents and grandparents, such that they became used to getting their own way and developed a sense of entitlement. The combined effect on their psyches of participation in the GPCR and being a single (male) child is evident in several of the leaders of modern China. It is transparent in their confidence in the ability to get what they seek, and in the ruthless manner in which such processes get carried out. The current supremo, General Secretary Xi, took charge in 2012 at a period when the PRC had already developed into a superpower and was rapidly catching up with the US. This may account at least in part for the transparency with which Xi has declared what the CPC's goals are, and in the manner in which military force has been used to try and secure what school textbooks in the PRC have long claimed to be the 'legitimate' borders of the PRC.[2] School texts in the PRC speak of much Indian and other territory (including the whole of Taiwan) as leftover bits and pieces needing to be integrated into the country. A mood of Manifest Destiny (especially after the 1997 handover by the UK of Hong Kong and the 2008 Summer Olympics in Beijing) has become manifest within party cadres, an emotion nurtured by the leadership. The nation has in large part come to accept the validity of the view of Chairman Mao and now forcefully and publicly articulated by General Secretary Xi of its rightful place at the head of the comity of nations. Not to mention the imperative of completing the 'unfinished' issue of the recovery of 'lost' territories. As long as fixed timelines were not thrown into the

---

[2] Ma Jian, 'Xi Jinping—a Son of the Cultural Revolution', *Japan Times*, May 15, 2016, https://www.japantimes.co.jp/opinion/2016/05/15/commentary/world-commentary/xi-jinping-son-cultural-revolution/.

mix, occasional references by PRC leaders to such 'unfinished' business did not cause much alarm, especially in countries that had been instrumental in ensuring the economic rise of China since the 1980s, in particular the US, Japan and Taiwan. It was only after Xi presented such intentions more publicly and emphatically than his immediate predecessors and speeded up the timetable for what had hitherto been a creeping annexation of fresh territories, that warning lights began flashing in world capitals about the direction the PRC was moving in. A direction that the CPC had its gaze on from its inception in 1921.

It was under Mao that the CPC ensured that the territory ruled from Beijing almost doubled in size from that run by its predecessors. This was through the inclusion of Xinjiang, Inner Mongolia and Manchuria in the 1940s and Tibet in the 1950s. There was almost no international resistance to such an expansion, not even from India, which through Beijing's takeover of Tibet suddenly acquired a long and at the time largely undefended border with the PRC. Or from the USSR so far as Xinjiang or Manchuria was concerned. General Secretary Hu Jintao (in whose period in office the overt and steady annexation of the South China Sea as part of the territory of the PRC began) and his successor, Xi, have thus far encountered very little global pushback in their annexation of the waters of the South China Sea. In accordance with his policy of accelerating the territorial sea and land changes that he regards as justifiable and inevitable, General Secretary Xi in his role as chairman of the CMC has ensured the creation of several artificial islands in the waters. Such structures have hampered freedom of navigation and cut into the lawful rights of the littoral states of the South China Sea over the waters now being claimed by the PRC. Such claims are a consequence of claiming ownership of the artificial islands created by Xi for this express purpose. To deter any effort of demolishing these structures, several of them are now populated by soldiers and other personnel with security-related functions. The construction of these artificial islands is designed to ensure that entry and exit points into and out of the South China Sea come under the control of the PLA, to the detriment of the sovereign rights of rightful claimants. Given such an artificially created reality, the coming period needs to witness the building of more such islands, including by the US and other members of the Quadrilateral Security Dialogue (India, Japan and Australia). However, as yet there has been no movement in such a necessary direction.

The South China Sea, Taiwan and the Himalayan massif are the three immediate territorial objectives of the CPC general secretary. Xi seeks to replicate the legacy of Chairman Mao by expanding the territory controlled by Beijing, whether these be in the sea, land or air. Taiwan has, as a consequence, seen a significant increase in probes by the PLA Air Force and Navy, with its sea and air space getting violated on a routine basis. The boundaries of 'normal' behaviour are being altered to Taiwan's disadvantage, as is the Line of Actual Control with India or the territorial waters of several of the members of the Association of Southeast Asian Nations (ASEAN). Given that such behaviour is outside the norm expected from a responsible member of the UN Security Council, it is increasingly likely that a PLA pilot may trigger an exchange of fire that may bring in the US and Japan, should the PRC respond to such an exchange over Taiwanese airspace in a disproportionate manner. As with the South China Sea, Xi's heightened resort to the military (backed by diplomacy of unprecedented verbal strength) has converted into a likely

theatre of kinetic action, land, air and sea space that in the
past was far removed from such a possibility.[3] Unlike his
predecessors, who appeared content to wait indefinitely before
seeking to enforce claims that lack international validity, Xi
Jinping is clearly a leader in a hurry to burnish what he sees as
his accomplishments and consequently his legacy. Now that
he has secured a record-breaking, rule-busting third five-year
term as CPC general secretary, Xi is under pressure to deliver
on such a mandate so as to accumulate backing for a fourth
term in 2027. In the way of what took place in the era of Mao
in the Korean peninsula, the probability is rising that the PLA
will be engaged in a kinetic exchange with the US and its allies
before the present term of the CPC general secretary ends.
Mao intervened in the Korean War confident in the backing
of what was then the USSR and is now Russia. Today, Xi is as
confident of Putin's backing for his warring against the island
country as Mao was of Stalin's support in his intervention
in the Korean civil war of the 1950s. Once such an exchange
takes place, where it will conclude is indeterminate. It is clear
that as with Mao, economic well-being of the people is less of
a priority in the policy calculus of the CPC leadership than
the enforcing of claims through the use or threat of use of
force. Till now, including in the case of the Spratly islands and
other such territories that have in effect been absorbed into
the PRC, unilateral resort to expansionary moves by the PLA
have met with almost no response from any other country,
barring verbal sallies that are clearly intended for domestic

---

[3] Murray Heibert, Phuong Nguyen and Gregory B. Poling, 'Perspectives
on the South China Sea: Diplomatic, Legal, and Security Dimensions of the
Report', Center for Strategic and International Studies, September 2014,
https://csis-website-prod.s3.amazonaws.com/s3fs-public/legacy_files/files/
publication/140930_Hiebert_PerspectivesSouthChinaSea_Web.pdf

audiences to believe that something is being done to counter such expansionism beyond verbiage.

Among the three theatres where kinetic exchanges between the PLA and other militaries is likely, there has already been a deadly clash in Galwan in 2020 across the Himalayas with the Indian Army. This was caused by PLA intrusions that year that were broader, deeper and involved far more forces than had been the case since the post-1962 border war. From the viewpoint of the long-term interests of the PRC, it would have made more sense to invest in building better relations with India rather than in seeking to constrain—in many ways contain— India by establishing relationships with its neighbours such as would promote that goal. The CPC leadership, influenced significantly by CMC groupthink, instead has chosen a path that is distinctly unhelpful to better Sino-Indian relations. Such policies include:

(a) Attempts to prevent India from emerging as an equal of the PRC, especially in defence capability and in economic performance. More than any other country in Asia, the country that has the inbuilt potential to replicate the success of China since the 1980s is India. Infirmities in the largely colonial-era governance construct have thus far inhibited such potential from getting actualized, but changes in the administrative and policy matrix would remove such a block. Rather than build up goodwill, it was deemed more advantageous by the CPC leadership to ensure through a multiplicity of ways that India drain away its potential through a hollowing out of its industry as a consequence of the replacement of domestically produced items with Chinese substitutes, and the infiltration of state structures to promote non-utilization of its natural resources to the extent made possible by the overall governance and societal structure in the country. In such a task, non-state actors have played a keystone role, often through courts or the media. Especially after 2004, there has been a significant shift from local production to reliance on imports from the PRC.

(b) PRC-controlled entities have been active, increasingly so in the blogosphere, to ensure that India remains chained to issues in South Asia rather than divert attention and resources to dealing with the threat from China. Within the country, they have sought to cultivate opposing voices in the policy and political discourse, so that once more, the concentration of effort is on fighting internal battles, rather than working towards any kind of coordination with like-minded powers against an external enemy. This has been aided by the manner in which the comprehensive warfare strategy adopted by the PRC (of carrying out 'attacks' on fronts as diverse as the media, politics, society and industry apart from the border), and which camouflages intentions and effects through a 'salami slicing' strategy on the border and recessed activity through multiple willing domestic cut-outs on other fronts.

(c) Xi Jinping has abandoned whatever pretence the PRC had of neutrality between Pakistan and India regarding Kashmir. The unveiling of the China-Pakistan Economic Corridor (the northern neck of which passed through Indian territory illegally occupied by Pakistan since 1948) was a non-verbal affirmation of the fact that CPC policy accepts the Pakistan military's case on Kashmir, which is that the entire state ought to be incorporated into Pakistan, a substantial chunk of which would subsequently be handed over to China, as has already been done by Pakistan in parts of Kashmir where it is under unlawful occupation. Recent maps, including some distributed during the 15–16 September 2022 Samarkand meeting of the Shanghai Cooperation Organisation, have shown Ladakh and Arunachal Pradesh as part of China, and Kashmir as forming part of Pakistan. Interestingly, changes in nomenclature into Mandarin variants of such territories have been copied by Russian analysts as well in place of the correct (Indian) nomenclature.

(d) Taking advantage of the silo system that marks the functioning of the Indian government, PRC interlocutors have tailored their actions and their messages in a manner that would secure optimum results for themselves from each silo in India. The boundary issue (presented as a dispute in India by the PRC side but within China as a matter that needs to be settled in the manner sought by the CPC) has been sought to be separated from questions of commerce. In effect, cash surpluses generated from trade with India (including through switch and smuggling methods) are being used to provide the means for the Pakistan military to continue with its campaign of seeking to kneecap India before the country reaches the level of GDP as would make it less vulnerable to external and externally induced domestic pressures and hostile actions. In a way, what is taking place is similar to 1947, when Mahatma Gandhi insisted that money be transferred to Pakistan at the precise period when the military of that country was taking the lives of both civilians and armed forces personnel in India through its invasion of Kashmir, including what is now Pakistan-occupied Kashmir and Gilgit-Baltistan, both belonging to India but occupied by Pakistan and partly by the PRC. The saintly Mahatma got his way, and money was handed over to Pakistan that was subsequently used against India.

Despite the CPC—especially the CMC—line of seeking to
kneecap India before it takes off into high and self-sustained
growth (to paraphrase Walt W. Rostow),[4] the hold of the colonial
construct and its accompanying mindset on the governance
structure of India has ensured that successive prime ministers
had fallen prey in some degree to the fantasy that India and
China can form their own G-2 in Asia, by stitching together
an alliance that would bring together 2.7 billion people into
a joint search for prosperity. Such an assumption (held only
by the Indian side despite being verbally affirmed to Indian
interlocuters by the PRC) falls to the ground when confronted
with the reality that the only G-2 that Beijing was willing to
accept (and that too on a temporary basis) was between China
and the US. Since Xi took charge, not even that. There is room
only for a unipolar world order, a G-1. In the CPC view, there
can only be a lone tiger on the Asian mountain, never two or
more, and that will need to be the PRC. It has been said by
Churchill, that America finally does the right thing, but only
after trying out all the other alternatives. The same could be
said for many other democracies. A like process appears to be
taking root in India, where finally the realities of geopolitical
currents are driving Indian policymakers towards the path that
needs to be taken, which is to create a chain of interlocking
alliances designed to ensure that the conflict with the PRC ends
not in the kneecapping of India but on a contrary result. And
working to ensure a decoupling of India's own supply chains
from China, besides attracting investment away from the PRC.

While the CPC speaks often of the divergences between
itself and political formations and policies within NATO,

---

[4]   Walt Whitman Rostow, *The Stages of Economic Growth* (Cambridge: Cambridge
University Press, 1991), https://doi.org/10.1017/CBO9780511625824.

especially the US, the reality is that much of the policies being formulated within Beijing are based on an exhaustive study of the past policy of countries such as the US or the UK during their prime until the middle of the previous century. The PLA, judging by its actions in various theatres, appears to have lifted not simply pages but chapters from US (and earlier UK) policy of relying on armed force to achieve the objectives set for it by the leadership. The CPC's propensity to adapt and adopt what regime analysts in the PRC believe to be the toolkit of the US ought not to come as a surprise, as the intention of the Chinese leadership is to replace Pax Americana with Pax Sinica, just as Pax Britannica was replaced during the course of the 1939–45 war by Pax Americana. The difference is that the changeover then was smooth, with the UK acquiescent in what it knew to be inevitable. The CPC leadership is aware that this time around, there may be resistance from Washington to efforts at its being replaced by Beijing as the global epicentre of authority. The earlier strategy is to ensure that the power differential reach such a level as to make resistance futile. Such a plan was proceeding smoothly so long as the 'final objective' of the CPC leadership was not obvious but has been facing increasing headwinds now that CPC General Secretary Xi Jinping has judged that the time for 'hiding one's strength and biding time' is over.

Apart from the onset of Cold War 2.0 between the PRC and the US, what may upset Xi's plans is what appears to be an obsessive focus on centralization in the office of the general secretary. Every subordinate source of authority has found its discretionary powers diminished, usually in practice but occasionally in a formal way as well. Decentralization of authority and giving confidence to lower levels to take decisions within a wide band of policy was a factor that drove the high growth engine of the PRC from 1983 to 2012, the year in which General Secretary Xi took over and began the work of consolidating his hold over the Party and the government that institution controls.[5] In such a process, the private sector had been a force multiplier, but since the advent of Xi, private industry has had to accept dictates and personnel given to it by the Party even on issues related to business decisions taken by subsidiaries in foreign locations.[6]

The apparent discord between Alibaba founder Jack Ma and Xi that surfaced in 2020 most probably arose when the former hesitated to rubber-stamp some of the demands made on his entities by elements in the PLA and the intelligence services. Obedience to such dictates, or even accepting many of the requisites of what in the Soviet Union were called the 'Organs' in the Stalin era, could lead to legal complications in several host countries that are important for the overall profitability of several Chinese versions of the Korean Chaebol. In effect, Chinese companies are being ordered by the CPC under Xi to act as the catspaw for the PRC, specifically the PLA, including by covertly handing over user data that the military may find of use. Jack Ma may have sought to demur, and more than his outsize public persona, this was probably what led to his eclipse from both public view as well as in the day-to-day operations of the enterprise he founded and ran expertly before the dust-up with Xi's underlings.[7]

---

[5] Bert Hofman, 'Reflections on 40 Years of China's Reforms,' in *China's 40 Years of Reform and Development: 1978-2018*, ed. Ross Garnaut, Ligang Song and Cai Fang (Acton: The Australian National University Press, 2018), 59.

[6] Nicholar Lardy, 'Private Sector Development', in *China's 40 Years of Reform and Development: 1978-2018*, ed. Ross Garnaut, Ligang Song and Cai Fang (Acton: The Australian National University Press, 2018), 338.

[7] Ryan McMorrow, 'The Vanishing Billionaire: How Jack Ma Fell Foul of Xi Jinping', *Financial Times*, April 15, 2021, https://www.ft.com/content/1fe0559f-de6d-490e-b312-abba0181da1f.

There was a time, especially during the decade when Jiang Zemin was CPC general secretary, when the Party did a lot of what its public and private businesses wanted the state to do. These days, Xi has ensured that the reverse is taking place. There is a difference between coordination between the government and the private sector (in the manner witnessed over decades in Japan and South Korea), and subordination of the latter to the former in the manner which took place in India under Nehru and Indira Gandhi. The Nehru model is now being tried out in steroidal form in Xi's China, where private companies are in effect being turned into subsidiaries of the state. Despite several tycoons joining the ranks of the 'party of peasants and workers' since the Jiang period, it is apparent from the web of policy directives in both implied as well as written form that merely being a CPC member is not sufficient, although it may be a necessary condition for prospering in the Xi era in a way that it earlier was not.

What is called for by the general secretary is complete acceptance of the dictates of the Party that get conveyed through the relevant units of that immense construct. As Jack Ma may some day testify, it is not enough that such fealty extends to 50 per cent or even 60 per cent of the Party's 'requests' being carried out by the private enterprise concerned. Anything below a level of obedience of close to 100 per cent is regarded as disloyalty and may be subject to the consequences inflicted for such a mindset and behaviour patterns. Especially given (i) the decoupling of several foreign advanced tech enterprises from the PRC and (ii) the shrinkage of the global market as a consequence of restrictions placed since Cold War 2.0 came into effect, the manner in which the private sector in China is getting its autonomy and authority eroded is likely to impact the growth that has for decades powered the expansion of PRC's external influence and domestic well-being.

The taking away of so much effective authority over decision-making involving matters of concern to the provinces and cities they are tasked to administer has resulted in a subterranean discontent against the CPC general secretary that could manifest in a much more visible manner should the decline in economic performance relative to past decades continue. Economic progress is judged not merely in absolute but in relative terms, and memories remain fresh of the days of Deng, Jiang and even Hu, when the autonomy of party cadres was substantial and the standard of living of the people rose in a manner not witnessed in the past, certainly not for the previous two centuries. Xi has understood the danger and has sought to combat it by boosting 'patriotic' feelings among the people, attempting to drill into them the perception that the hardships they have begun to face are not the result of CPC policies but the consequence of the hostility of countries that are envious about China's rise and who seek to throttle this. Given Xi's reliance on the military as the enforcer of diplomacy, it would not be unusual for several within the PRC (including the CPC) to believe that much of the fissures with outside powers that are being witnessed since the onset of Cold War 2.0 are not so much the consequence of the PLA-influenced policies of General Secretary Xi towards several countries, including the US and India, but active sabotage of Xi's policies by such powers. At the same time, the risks are considerable for the assumed securing of public support through a major victory in the field, such as the capture of Taiwan or a repeat of the humiliation inflicted on India in 1962. Should conditions continue to deteriorate, impacting Xi's support among the people and the cadre, this may be an option that the CPC leadership core may regard as a necessary exercise for domestic reasons of public acquiescence to dictatorship and their continued cooperation.

The problem facing Xi is that the population of the PRC in the twenty-first century is very different from what it was in the first half of the twentieth, and repeating the experiments and slogans of the Mao period may not work as well this time around. Unlike during that time, there is no longer a fear among large swathes of the population that their country is under threat from outside. Quite the reverse in fact, given the manner in which the perception of the undoubted rise of the PRC into superpower status has been disseminated and mainstreamed. Neither are there vivid memories of mass starvation and deprivation, which is why hardship that would have seemed trifling in the 1950s may soon be a cause for public discontent. Visible declines in living standards may cause social eruptions that the leadership may judge can be met only by an external show of force and a military triumph, such as the takeover of Taiwan or an attempted 1962-style humiliation of India by seizing Arunachal and Ladakh. Such a contingency may explain the preparatory build-up across both the Taiwan and Himalayan theatres by the PLA. This suggests a possible involvement of that force once ordered by the general secretary to create a diversion designed to quell domestic unrest caused by some of his policies.

3

Russia Seemingly Content
with Half a Loaf

While the Russian Federation has a dollar GDP much lower than
that of India, the moves made on the geopolitical chessboard
by President Vladimir V. Putin have ensured that its weightage
in the global system is substantially more than what it was
under Boris Yeltsin. It was during the latter period of the rule
of Mikhail Gorbachev's term as CPSU general secretary (1985–
91) that the Soviet government, in effect, downgraded the
importance of India in its global calculus. However, individual
Soviet citizens (with a depth of commitment that is among the
extraordinary qualities of the Russian people) ensured that
technological cooperation in particular continued to take place
despite frowns from Washington. The collapse of the USSR
by the close of 1991 substantially lessened such collaboration,
as what may be described as the mafia elements around
President Yeltsin ensured that Moscow became subservient
to Washington. However, even during this period, once again
individual Russian scientists ensured a modicum of cooperation
between themselves and their Indian counterparts. In several
fields, it was not the Russian side but dubious elements within
the Indian polity and bureaucracy that facilitated the Central

Intelligence Agency (CIA), in particular, in operations designed to gut the cryogenic engine programme of the Indian Space Research Organisation (ISRO).

The fabricated case built by elements in the Intelligence Bureau and the Kerala Police against key space scientists working on the cryogenic engine programme delayed its completion by over a decade.[1] Overall, India did not reap the benefits expected from the gesture of the Narasimha Rao government to put an artificially high value of the rupee for the Russian rouble as the benchmark for repayments of Soviet-era loans by India, rather than repay such debts through taking advantage of the low rate of the rouble following the advent to power of Yeltsin in 1992. The rupee-rouble agreement (1993) represented in effect an outright gift of over $9 billion over time to the Russian Federation from a country that had—and still has—the largest number of desperately poor people in the world. While the Russian Federation under Yeltsin and a handful of commercial enterprises in both countries that were linked to India-Russia trade benefited, the people of India lost through this show of generosity. An action not repeated by any other country that had Soviet-era debts, which several repudiated in full. Not that the interests of the people of India have been much more than a merely verbal or nominal priority for some of the policymakers in the Lutyens Zone of Delhi.

As was obvious from the very start of Yeltsin's overlordship of Russia, he had accepted a position of subservience to the US that made earlier Russian tech collaboration with India problematic and in many ways impossible to continue. This was the consequence of the restrictive policies adopted by the Clinton administration towards India, ironically during the

---

[1] 'ISRO Case Scuttled Cryogenic Engine Development, Says Former Scientist', *The Hindu*, 24 June 2016, https://www.thehindu.com/news/cities/Kochi/isro-case-scuttled-cryogenic-engine-development-says-former-scientist/article5062224.ece.

very period when the White House was lavishing favours on Beijing, including in tech. Given such interlocking realities, the 1993 Indo-Russian agreement setting a grossly overvalued price for the rouble for the purposes of loan repayment represents another of the numerous decisions taken within the Lutyens Zone that need examination and accountability, but which has almost entirely escaped the former and entirely the latter. A recent example of unilateral largesse is what was carried out in February 2021 on the Sino-Indian border. This was the withdrawal of Indian troops from the Kailash Heights in the Himalayan massif despite there being no countervailing concession made by the PLA on the sectors where it was menacing Indian forces. In effect, the Line of Actual Control has been changed by the PLA in a manner unfavourable to India, and not for the first time. Judging by the tenor of remarks being made by External Affairs Minister S. Jaishankar about the Sino-Pakistan alliance, it appears to have been accepted within South Block that the many unilateral concessions made by successive governments in the past were a mistake.

Unlike the USSR, the successor Russian Federation is no longer accepted as a superpower. However, its territorial spread combined with the ingenuity of its people is likely to ensure that Moscow enters the superpower ranks later, after India makes the grade. The Atlantic Alliance, on account of its continuing hostile policy towards Russia even after the break-up of the USSR in 1992, has practically eliminated the possibility of Moscow joining hands with Washington and its EU partners in an alliance designed to slow down the Chinese drive for a new unipolar world led by Beijing. Such a coming together of Russia and the US and allies within the Eurasian land mass would have given the Atlantic Alliance two more decades of primacy during the initial decades of the twenty-first century before being overtaken by the Indo-Pacific as the global centre point of gravity. That was not to be. Despite this, the manner of prosecution of the 2022 war in Ukraine by NATO is indicative of its belief that the Atlantic Alliance is still the pivot of global geopolitics, when with the 2008 global financial crash, that position shifted to the Indo-Pacific, with China replacing Russia as the primary threat.

During Cold War 1.0, the US and China battled the USSR together. In Cold War 2.0, China and Russia are jointly ranged against the US.

Perceptions of Atlanticist capabilities are different from the expansive thinking within the Atlantic Alliance. In 2022, the Sino-Russian alliance has been set in stone by the policies being followed by key members of NATO, an organization that acts as though it was still Moscow that was foe number one rather than Beijing. During the 1990s, President Clinton's policy towards Russia continued much of the Cold War 1.0 thinking that saw Moscow not as a prospective ally but still an adversary.

The effort of the Clinton administration was to hollow out Russian capabilities in technology and manufacturing, a task that appears to have been facilitated by Yeltsin and his indifferent attitude towards any interests other than those relating to his family and friends. The members of the Atlantic Alliance were of course eager to indulge such 'friends and family', as through them they could weaken the capacity of the Russian Federation to continue as a significant generator of technology and manufacturing, especially in matters concerning the military. Russia became dependent on the export of raw materials, principally petro products, a situation that the wall of sanctions imposed since 2008 by the Atlantic Alliance against Russia has perpetuated. Clinton's planned diminution of the industrial capacity of Russia proceeded in lockstep with the boost given by the White House to the development of similar capacity in a country that poses a much more potent threat to the primacy of the US, and which raises the risk of the eclipse of Europe greater than Russia ever did. This is the PRC. To this day, action on the China front, in contrast to that against Russia has been hesitant and insufficient.

Under CPC General Secretary Hu Jintao, and much more vigorously under his successor Xi Jinping, Beijing has followed a policy of working together with those elements of industry, science and agriculture in Russia that are helpful to its own progress. In the process, although not on the scale of the transfer of technologies from the US and the EU to the PRC since the 1980s, several technologies and processes have been transferred from Russia to China. The eventual aim of Beijing is the same as Washington's was under President Clinton, which is to convert Russia into a pastoral country whose manufacturing capabilities get replaced with units springing up elsewhere. However, this is being done in a manner far more nuanced and subtle than the obvious efforts at dilution of technologies in Russia that are made by the US and its partners in the EU. The pairing of Moscow and Beijing has intensified since Putin took over the leadership of his country in 1999.

Through his first three years in office, although in an increasingly sceptical manner (given the lack of response from the US and the EU, who had become used to the servile behaviour of the Yeltsin team), Putin sought better relations with the US and the EU in tones reminiscent of the 'Common European Home' refrain of Mikhail Gorbachev. The problem facing Putin was that neither the US, Germany, the UK or France wanted Russia in either the EU or NATO. They were aware that the entry of Moscow would severely impact their own individual influence within the councils of both these entities. Just as

China is hostile to the growth into full potential of India for fear that Delhi would displace Beijing in Asia's pecking order, so is the US concerned about Russia, aware that that country has the potential to replace US primacy in Europe with its own, if given a chance at unfettered growth and access to technology in the manner in which the PRC was given a chance earlier.

While what is described as the St Petersburg school among policymakers in Moscow believes Russia to be part of Europe, despite its being in possession of half of the Asian land mass, the Russian Federation may be more accurately described as different from both Asia as well as Europe. Russia is neither—it is a fully Eurasian power just as the US is effectively a quadri-continental power, with China seeking to displace it. As a Eurasian great power, the Russian Federation is well positioned to take advantage of the synergy contained in the working together of Europe and Asia. Given the increasing closeness between Beijing and Moscow, it is probable that the policy of expansion of PRC exclusivist power into Europe and Central Asia will to an extent be camouflaged by CPC General Secretary Xi sufficiently to present the appearance of a sharing of the spoils between the two partners of the Sino-Russian alliance.

A sharing of at least some of the geopolitical benefits would ensue through the numerous bonds between the two countries that have been created by Xi Jinping and Vladimir Putin. Such linkages will only multiply, should the duo continue to rule their respective countries for a decade more. Just as the window to divest North Korea of its nuclear weapons by force appears to have been passed, so too do the events of 2022 related to Ukraine appear to have shut the door towards a rapprochement between the Atlantic Alliance and the Russian Federation. This is a consequence of not merely the policies pursued by the Kremlin, but also because of the policies towards Russia of the US in particular. These are policies that are grounded in the continuing hold of Cold War 1.0 Atlanticists in foreign and security policy formulation in Washington and London in particular. A genuine partnership between the Russian Federation and the US was possible during the Clinton administration, but disappeared completely by 2003, the period when Putin began to put aside the Europeanist theories of the St Petersburg school. By 2006, he had accepted that the EU and NATO would never reconcile to a partnership with Russia. From then onwards, whether in Georgia, Crimea or elsewhere, the actions of Russia under Putin have been predictable, given the geopolitical situation faced by it. With each turn of the sanctions lever, the impetus towards an alliance with Beijing became stronger in Moscow.

Given the overall geopolitical situation, there was no other viable option for Putin than to respond to the overtures of Xi, despite the success of the PRC in replacing several of the lines of manufactures of the Russian Federation with its own enterprises. In the evolving global order of the twenty-first century, it is no longer possible to align with the Atlantic Alliance and at the same time retain in-depth collaborative relations with the PRC, or to align with China and despite that, maintain close ties with the Atlantic Alliance.

The decision to move closer to China was in substantial part made for the Russian Federation by the policies initiated by President Clinton and since then followed by every one of his successors. A temporary exception was Trump, who understood with the street-smart savvy of the New York builder that delinking Moscow and perhaps even Pyongyang from the orbit of Beijing's strategic objectives would sharply constrain the PRC's ability to alter global geopolitics. US President Richard Nixon, during his tenure between 1969 and

1974, had harnessed the PRC against the USSR. However, the Cold War 1.0 school of strategy still influential in Washington, New York and elsewhere, joined hands with fellow travellers in key capitals in Europe (among which Warsaw was among the most emphatic). This was to ensure that President Trump was stopped at the initial stages in efforts of the White House that were aimed at ensuring a Roosevelt-Stalin model reset of relations between Moscow and Washington so as to confront the primary threat. Perhaps all to the good, as by the time Trump took office in 2017, the Sino-Russian alliance had hardened into a construct that would be almost impossible to dissolve. Had President Trump continued on a trajectory of holding the PRC accountable and constraining it, the likelihood is that it would have been obvious to him that it was too much of an ask. As matters stand, with his choice of Cold War 1.0 veteran Atlanticists such as John Bolton, Steve Mnuchin and General McMaster to populate his government, his outreach to Moscow went nowhere almost from the start.

There has been much talk in the capitals of NATO about Russia 'not following international norms'. These refer to the rules set by the Atlantic Alliance for countries outside this charmed circle. Even Japan, despite its efforts in the pre-Shinzo Abe era of seeking to convert itself into a part of Europe that had somehow drifted into a corner of Asia, has not been brought into the Atlanticist club, as for example, witness its exclusion from the talks that preceded the signing of the Joint Comprehensive Plan of Action (JCPOA) with Iran in 2015. If Germany was allowed entry into the team negotiating with Iran without being a member of the UNSC P-5, why was Japan not included? Given the manner in which NATO continues to regard itself primarily as a bulwark of offence and defence not against China but Russia, a policy continued by President

Clinton and followed by his successors (with the attempted exception of Trump), it was no surprise that post-2006, Putin decided that Moscow should retake the Crimea and earlier, enforce a more acceptable (to Russia) territorial alignment in Georgia.

It ought to have come as no surprise when Putin has recognized the breakaway regions of Luhansk and the Donbass (in Ukraine) as independent countries. The harder the sanctions screw gets turned on Russia, the more it will exhibit the behaviour of the outsider, the way in which it has been treated even after 1991. It is a reality of the present that objective conditions no longer justify the Atlantic Alliance, regarding it as axiomatic that countries follow agreements and conditions that it itself or its sheet anchor, the US, flouts, an example being the JCPOA with Iran. Once it was scrapped, Iran resumed its path towards nuclear capability. When President Trump walked away from the agreement with Iran rather than continuing with the terms of an agreement that had been signed by the US, both Germany and France in effect followed in their actions the example of the US, all the while demanding that Iran should remain tethered to a deal that was no longer being followed by almost all other signatories. The Atlanticist insistence (some would say illusion) is that the Russian Federation should ignore the eastward expansion of NATO and put itself in the same position as the country was under Yeltsin. This is of being supine in the face of kinetic actions against its remaining allies by Atlantic Alliance partners, as for example what took place in the detachment by military force of Kosovo in 2008 from the Serbian Federation. This was preceded by the earlier bombing of Serbia in 1999 by NATO. This was under the prodding of the UK and Germany, the latter country having been fought with courage and persistence by the Serbians during the 1938–45 war initiated by Hitler. Such behaviour by the Serbs contrasted with the Croats, many of whom favoured Hitler's side and had little hesitation in making such a preference obvious in battle and in the commission of atrocities, until it became clear by the close of 1943 that the Axis was doomed. A slice of history that the UK forgot in its obsession with the 'liberation' of Kosovo, thereby creating the very same template being used by President Putin to justify his takeover of territories in Ukraine since 2014.

Yeltsin's subservience to Washington resulted in the Kremlin abandoning its long-standing role as protector of the Serbian people against external attack. More recently, in the conflict over Nagorno-Karabakh between Azerbaijan and Armenia, it was deference to Beijing that persuaded Moscow to go along with China, Pakistan and Turkey in divesting Armenia (a country with which Moscow had a security treaty) of substantial chunks of territory that had earlier been within the control of Yerevan. It would have been a simple matter to use the military assets of the Russian Federation sufficiently to ensure that this control got retained despite the campaign waged by Azerbaijan with assistance from Pakistan and Turkey, both close to the PRC. The 'all-weather' relationship between China and Pakistan in particular will be a growing problem for Russia, in that the Pakistan Army will continue, along with Turkey and China, to empower groups that seek to radicalize the populations of Central Asia and Azerbaijan. Such planting of the seeds of extremism must already be taking place in that largely moderate country, with the full backing of Turkey, whose head of state has become among the top leaders of the Wahhabi International, now that Saudi Arabia under the influence of Crown Prince Mohammed bin Salman is moving away from that creed.

Azerbaijan may have won some territory in Nagorno-Karabakh, but it may have cause to regret the fact that subsequent efforts at radicalization within its population are ongoing by Turkey and Pakistan.[2] As will Russia, now that it is in danger of ceding primacy in the Central Asian republics that were once part of the USSR to China, which is the primary force multiplier for General Headquarters (GHQ) Rawalpindi and facilitator of the Wahhabi cause in several locations, except of course within its own shores.

It was Charles de Gaulle who kept France's independence of action intact while joining the Atlantic Alliance, thereby showing that it was entirely possible for an ally to have its own mind and consequently policy on selected issues while being anchored to the fundamentals of an alliance system. The Gaullist version of alliance was followed later by President Jacques Chirac, who braved the ire of President George W. Bush for opposing his 2003 campaign against Iraq under Saddam Hussein and provides a template for the US-India Indo-Pacific alliance. The fundamental objective of the alliance is to ensure a free and open Indo-Pacific (a formulation which added the word 'inclusive', which Prime Minister Modi added in 2018 at the Shangri-la dialogue) and to resist efforts of domination by China. This common objective must be ensured through cooperation between Delhi and Washington (along with other powers having a similar objective, such as Canberra and Tokyo). At the same time, on issues of secondary importance, the perspectives of the US and India may differ in the manner that those of France and the US differed, most visibly during the

---

[2] 'Armenia-Azerbaijan Ceasefire Fails Again, Thanks to Pakistan, Turkey', *Business Standard*, October 19, 2020, https://www.business-standard.com/article/international/armenia-azerbaijan-ceasefire-fails-again-thanks-to-pakistan-turkey-120101901246_1.html.

periods when Jacques Chirac refused to join in the war begun by Bush and his UK counterpart Tony Blair to rid the world of Saddam Hussein.

Partly due to policy missteps and an inability to seize the opportunities opened by the collapse of the USSR by the US and its key European partners, the Sino-Russian alliance has become a reality in the twenty-first century, and in this, developments in Azerbaijan as well as the manner in which Moscow is echoing Beijing's criticism of the Quad, as well as the broader Indo-Pacific strategy of the democracies, indicates that the relationship of the Russian Federation to the PRC is unequal if not wholly subservient. Thus far, the fault lines within the alliance, such as Beijing's boost to the Wahhabi International and its effort to replace Russia as the primary outside power in Central Asia, have yet to be exploited by the Atlanticists, who continue to follow a policy that overall has been helpful to Beijing.

It is clear that President Putin and his advisers believe that Russia at present has more to gain from the Sino-Russian alliance than if they were to distance themselves from it. The alliance ensures for Russia a goodly share (likely 30:70) of the geopolitical gains that may potentially accrue to the PRC should it prevail in Cold War 2.0. The option of repeating in reverse the Chinese Cold War 1.0 example of joining hands with the US against Russia with a coming together of Russia and the US in opposition to the PRC's expansionism has been foreclosed by the policy errors by the Atlantic powers and the continuing hold of concepts formulated during the post-1945 period of ascendancy of the Atlantic Alliance. Despite such denial, the realities of Cold War 2.0 are becoming more and more apparent. This has given an opening to India to 'do a China on China' during the new Cold War by aligning with the US to possibly prevent the PRC from establishing its dominance over the Indo-Pacific region. Even where investment in new enterprises is concerned, companies are not likely to move from China except to a country that they know to be a willing and reliable partner of the US and its allies now that the world has entered the era of Cold War 2.0. Subtle hints and double *entendres* may not be sufficient for India to generate such a perception among investors and possible partner countries.

The Sino-Russian alliance has given Moscow diplomatic and other cover sufficient to enable a ramping up of activities in the European theatre, especially where the Baltic states and countries such as Ukraine, Belarus and Georgia are concerned. At the same time, it gives a similar boost to Beijing's efforts at securing primacy over the decision-making process in South Asia and the ASEAN region, especially its efforts at hobbling India, a country with the potential to not just equal but overtake the PRC in comprehensive national power in coming decades. Indeed, the managing of what may be called the 'India Account' is an important component of the Sino-Russian alliance, with Moscow expected to work towards ensuring that relations between Washington and Delhi do not reach the stage of an effective military partnership against the efforts of the PRC to secure primacy and later hegemony over the Indo-Pacific. Such hegemony is the objective of the CPC as is clear from the assertiveness of its claims over vast tracts of the Himalayan massif, the South China Sea and Taiwan. The peremptory way in which countries neighbouring the PRC are being treated indicates that the CPC Standing Committee, headed by Xi Jinping and since October 2022 comprising wholly his supporters, is confident that Pax Sinica will replace Pax Americana before Xi leaves office after what he expects to be his fourth and final term as CPC general secretary. The ambitions of the Russian Federation, now that it has undergone the trauma suffered by the people as a consequence of the man-made disruption of the Gorbachev and Yeltsin years, is relatively more modest. It is to reassert Russian primacy in those regions that were once part of the USSR in Europe, and to hold back attempts at encroachment by the Atlantic Alliance of what the Kremlin defines as its interests and rights in these regions.

Russia was once a superpower and seeks to join the US, China and subsequently India in a twenty-first-century version of the Big Four. Over time, as its economy catches its breath and its technology (and manufacturing) sectors regain some of their earlier potency, Moscow hopes to establish the same relationship with Beijing that Delhi is developing with Washington, or in a manner similar to the model fashioned by de Gaulle of France—an ally but with a mind and will of its own where some matters are concerned. The problem facing the Kremlin is what seems to be an expanding appetite on the part of General Secretary Xi for establishing the 'Jhimi' system on a global basis, where Beijing would respect in protocol terms the leaderships of other countries, provided they in turn went by the dictates of China. Especially since 2012, when Xi Jinping took office, this is an expanding list, and in a less obvious way includes Russia as well. Mao did not accept the USSR's primacy in matters to do with the global communist movement, and neither will Putin accept the PRC's efforts at crafting a unipolar world. What Moscow seeks is a world with four poles: Moscow, Washington, Beijing and Delhi, with the other three opposing the US. Given that CPC policy, especially under Xi, would make any partnership between Delhi and Beijing harmful to the overall interests of India, what is likely is that there will be a US-India and a China-Russia pairing, with India backing the US in

Indo-Pacific but not always in Atlanticist policies that prioritize
Europe over Asia.

Until primacy is won in the Indo-Pacific over the US and
its partners, the PRC does not need to concentrate its focus
on Europe. This has given President Putin leeway in holding
his own within parts of Eurasia vis-à-vis his much more
economically advanced partner. The Asian part is different,
and specifically the Middle East and Central Asia, which
was part of the USSR until its collapse in 1991. The PRC
seeks primacy there by superseding the Russian Federation,
and Moscow's steady loss of influence in both regions to its
presumed ally must rankle within the Kremlin. As must be
the stealthy encroachment of vast tracts of Siberia (especially
near the border with China) by PRC citizens who are clearly
settling there on a permanent basis, changing demographics in
the manner that happened in Xinjiang and Tibet earlier, albeit
this time in a less overt and more cautious fashion. About two
decades ago, the present writer had suggested that the Russian
Federation invite immigrants from India to settle in Siberia.
This would have diluted the influence of settlers from the PRC
and enabled the central authorities in Moscow to retain control
over every part of this vast territory. Unlike settlers who are
from China, those from India have zero intention of altering
the control of Moscow over these regions. The suggestion was
not met with any action on the Russian side, even as migration
from the PRC into Russia (mainly the borderlands of Siberia)
has increased without pause.

Xi has doubled down on the gamble that successive leaders
of the PRC have taken in their dealings with the Pakistan Army,
which is that (a) it will continue to ensure a level of harassment to
India that would distract the bigger country from concentrating
on the threat from the PRC and (b) that it would continue to

maintain effective control over the people and the machinery of government in Pakistan and (c) keep the country stable and welcoming to Chinese interests. Later on, the expectation is that Russia will increasingly become as compliant with PRC dictates as Pakistan. In the case of Azerbaijan, Beijing made Moscow abandon the interests of Yerevan to those of Baku, another city that had once formed part of the USSR. In that conflict, Pakistan and Turkey were on the side of Azerbaijan, while Armenia was alone. In recent times, Xi Jinping has sought to ensure that Putin devote more attention to the security interests not just of the PRC but partly those of its 'all weather friend', the Pakistan military. This process has been taking place since 2015, and at the expense of India. Fortunately for Moscow, the Lutyens Zone is not known for adeptness in picking up early warnings and has put Russian overtures to GHQ Rawalpindi in the same benign light as Delhi's own earlier persistent efforts at changing the behaviour of GHQ Rawalpindi towards India through the giving of concessions to Pakistan that are both substantive as well as diplomatic.

Such an enforced union of Russian and Pakistani interests has led to the Kremlin having to ignore the lessons of the past (including those still relevant) and going along with Beijing's policy of cozying up to the Taliban in yet another gesture of appeasement towards GHQ Rawalpindi that will have consequences in Central Asia and later in Chechnya (a republic of Russia) that may prove difficult to reverse. Given the experience of the population of Afghanistan with Taliban rule, a better course would be to join hands with India and possibly Iran in extending support to the elements to oppose the Taliban. The entry of that entity into Kabul during August 2021 was a disaster for the people of Afghanistan, who have suffered since the 1960s through missteps made by the big owers in dealing with their country. By having an approach towards Afghanistan and Central Asia that is different from China and its Pakistan fixation that is a part of the structure of the Sino-Wahhabi alliance, Russia under President Putin is more in step with India where the growing Wahhabi influence in Afghanistan and Central Asia is concerned. Such a limited pairing of interests may be able to resist the efforts of Beijing to pull Russia closer to the Sino-Wahhabi alliance, and to work in concert with it, rather than insisting on a separate Sino-Russian alliance that does not include the Wahhabi component. For China of course, Wahhabism is welcome, except within the PRC. The ideal formation for Beijing would be a merger of the Sino-Wahhabi and Sino-Russian alliance, something that may already be happening in the form of covert efforts used by Russia to cause problems in Atlanticist countries through empowering Wahhabi elements in the manner that Beijing has long been doing through cut-outs such as Pakistan, Somalia and possibly now Turkey.

In the case of India, it is less adverse objective conditions than errors in policy formulation and execution that have held the country back. The situation confronting President Putin is different, in that there are structural issues that relate not just to the Soviet era but to the disastrous years under Yeltsin. While the economic (statist) polices pursued by the USSR may be responsible for much of the under-performance of Russia relative to its peers, the sanctions imposed by the Atlantic Alliance have exacted a heavy toll. While much of this was seemingly dismantled while the Russian Federation was under Yeltsin, in reality, what was done was to ensure an open door especially for US financial institutions, which benefited from an accommodative attitude to their moneymaking during the Yeltsin years (1992–99). Far from getting any benefit from the supposed relaxation of Atlanticist sanctions under President Yeltsin, the population of the Russian Federation underwent a steep fall in living standards during this period that has persisted in a significant part of the population to this day. From the 1990s, a few with connections to the government enriched themselves and their patrons. A few saw themselves as not merely paymasters but masters, such as Mikhail Khodorkovsky, who took on Vladimir Putin in 2003 (when he had an estimated wealth in excess of $15 billion), and as a consequence was deprived of not just his businesses but his freedom. Fortunately for him, once it was clear that he was no longer a threat to the regime, Khodorkovsky was freed and soon settled in the UK, where he had put away a little under $1 billion that had of course been undeclared to the Russian authorities. This has enabled him and his family to enjoy a comfortable lifestyle in London, a city that has for long enthusiastically welcomed those with substantial wealth no matter what their geopolitical interests and collateral pursuits are.

Vladimir Putin took charge as the President of the Russian Federation in 1999 and had begun to understand by the close of 2003 that there was no likelihood of Russia being welcomed into the 'common European family'. Such an integration had been the quest of CPSU General Secretary Mikhail S. Gorbachev, and expectations of such a 'homecoming' lingered in the St Petersburg school of strategic thinking in the Russian Federation, unlike the more Eurasian-oriented Moscow school. Subsequently, accepting that Russia had been and would remain a target of NATO and hostile commercial and diplomatic measures by the Atlantic Alliance powers, Putin, from 2006, took steps to shore up the defences of his country, including through intervening to prevent the creation of another hostile frontier in the east of Ukraine including through the recovery of Crimea, a territory that had earlier not been part of Ukraine but which had been transferred to it by an order of the presidium of the Soviet Union in 1954. Had Crimea become a NATO base in the manner sought by prominent Ukrainian politicians, the security of Putinist Russia would have been severely compromised. In 2014, Putin in effect detached the Donbass and Luhansk from Ukraine, thereby creating a buffer zone to the east, just in case Ukraine joined hands with NATO. Such measures resulted in Atlantic Alliance partners placing additional sanctions on Russia. Measures that were designed to shrink the economy and thereby increase pain for the public in the expectation that this would result in turmoil on the streets as had been witnessed in parts of the Middle East and Europe earlier in this century.

It was not unexpected that such punitive measures would steer Russia more into China's way, but the Atlanticist calculation was that economic enervation, and the resultant social unrest would prevent Moscow from being as potent a force multiplier as its potential entitled it to be. The problem is that Putin has not been showing signs of the Brezhnev-Gorbachev syndrome of abstaining from kinetic attacks on allies of the Atlantic powers that was demonstrated in the absence of any retaliation on Pakistan despite GHQ Rawalpindi acting as the force multiplier for the fighters battling the occupying Russian forces in Afghanistan. Should this understanding of Putin's difference with his predecessors not dawn, the risk to the Baltic states from a Russian invasion would be real. It is not only Ukraine that is in the sights of Russia under Putin.

Will the half loaf offered by the PRC continue to satisfy the Russian bear? It will as long as there is nothing better on offer. Several of Moscow's interests diverge from those of Beijing, and yet geopolitical compulsions are impelling the Kremlin to frame policies that mesh closely with the interests of the PRC in a manner less than ideal where the interests of the Russian Federation are involved. Changes in policy by the members of the Atlantic Alliance, in particular, would be needed to ensure that Moscow's dependence on Beijing diminish. As with the path of North Korea and since the scrapping of the JCPOA of Iran towards a nuclear weapon, soon it may become impossible to ensure what ought to be regarded as a necessity in the era of Cold War 2.0. This is to break the pairing between Russia and China, which alas, seems destined to endure.

4

India's 'Strategic Ambivalence' Constrains and Confuses

Had India's first deputy prime minister, Sardar Vallabhbhai Patel, been around until the mid-1960s, the country would have remained on the post-1945 track of becoming the biggest economy in Asia by the 1970s. This progression was stifled by the downsizing of private initiative under the now unbridled prime minister, Jawaharlal Nehru, who saw in the Soviet model of central planning and state control of industry the path needed to be taken by India. Given that oversized tranches of power to officials and politicians who supervised them looked attractive, this was a policy continued by his successor, Indira Gandhi, whose belief that democracy hindered progress in India had been made explicit in her interview to Italian journalist Oriana Fallaci.[1] While there were efforts at reform during the Rajiv Gandhi period, and even under the short-lived tenure of Chandra Shekhar, it was only post the 1991 liberalization that the reforms introduced in industrial licensing by Narasimha Rao effected an overall change in the outlook of the

---

[1] Indira Gandhi: Interviewed by Orianna Fallaci, Part 1, https://sangam.org/indira-gandhi-interviewed-orianna-fallaci/.

Government of India from 'Private business is evil' to 'Private business is good'. The reforms made by Rao were sufficient to place the country on a higher growth trajectory. The attacks on Rao's economic reforms from within the Congress Party since 1994 that were led by politicians close to Sonia Gandhi made the prime minister apply the brakes to further moves at reform after his political hold over the Congress Party began weakening in 1994. This was the consequence of his critics in the party allying with political and economic interests who were against the reforms, including some business interests who were averse to a more open economy. Such a deceleration of the reform process was visible in the final two years of his term (1991–96). Ultimately, the split in the Congress Party which took place just before the Lok Sabha elections that was engineered by Arjun Singh and N.D. Tiwari, two leaders close to Sonia Gandhi, helped ensure the defeat of the party in the 1996 Lok Sabha polls, and the beginning of an era of coalition governments that ended only with Narendra Modi's securing of a majority in the Lok Sabha in the 2014 polls, a feat repeated by him in 2019.

After Rao, there were sporadic attempts by his successors to reconstruct the governance and regulatory framework in India to incentivize initiative and enterprise, and thereby generate growth. A combination of crony capitalists and rent-seeking officials unwilling to let go of their powers of control and thereby extortion ensured that such efforts never progressed to the transformative level needed to generate what W.W. Rostow called 'the take-off into self-sustained (high) growth'. Nehru deserves much more attention in the field of his economic theories than he has received, given that he was the pioneer of a hybrid model that combined democracy in political choice with Soviet-style statism in the economic sphere. Apart from the economy, the foundations of Indian foreign policy were set by Nehru, once the first prime minister of the Republic of India assumed unchallenged supremacy over the Congress Party by 1951 with the demise of Deputy Prime Minister Vallabhbhai Patel. As prime minister, Nehru in large part assumed that countries such as Pakistan and China as neighbours would share India's Gandhian belief of non-violence and in the avoidance of the military as an instrument of statecraft, despite moves in the opposite direction from Rawalpindi and Beijing. The prime minister believed that even if they were initially hostile towards India, as Pakistan from the start visibly was, both would soon accept his undoubtedly accurate point of view, which was that peace was a better way forward than conflict.

This postulate was applied to policy towards both China and Pakistan, despite each having taken over large tracts of Indian territory. The fact that the ideology of the CPC would never accept India as anything other than a rival to be kept in check, or that the interests of the Pakistan military mandated constant tension with India, failed to appeal to him. Given his pacifist mindset, security and defence policy was not the priority for Prime Minister Nehru in the way that his economic and foreign policy were.

Terms such as 'Strategic Autonomy' and 'Strategic Ambiguity' are often used as justifications by those tasked to implement the broadly Nehruvian construct of foreign and security policy of India, and there remain many who extol their postulates as translated into policy while glossing over the consequences. What has been carried out by India since the 1950s may be better described as a policy of Strategic Ambivalence, for in a situation where low growth rates and an absence of self-reliance in many essentials, talk of 'Strategic Autonomy' was illusory. A shift in one direction of policy towards a world power was often followed by moves to a rival power. This was confusing to many, especially to the Great Powers, and resulted in almost all of them having superficially warm relations with India that avoided any automatic coming to the assistance of Delhi even when that was badly required, as for example during the 1962 border conflict with China. Fortunately, there did occur periods when ambivalence was put away and a clear choice made, such as the Indo-Soviet treaty signed in 1972 that was masterminded by Durga Prasad Dhar. The Indo-Soviet treaty staved off both PRC intervention in the 1971 war with Pakistan, as well as reducing the risk of falling prey to Nixon-Kissinger intimidation designed to make India desist from carrying forward its attack on the genocidal Pakistan Army of occupation in what was soon to become Bangladesh. Nixon and Kissinger acted in concert with the PRC and with Pakistan, and it was during that conflict that the Sino-Pakistan alliance established deep roots. GHQ Rawalpindi was defeated because of the kinetic operations conducted by the armed forces of the Republic of India and the Mukti Bahini, intervention that was intended to rescue Bangladesh from Pakistan military oppression and genocide. Unfortunately, the traditional post-1947 policy of 'let's give Pakistan another chance' went into operation after the conflict and prevented the holding to account of at least a few of the more genocidal commanders of the Pakistan Army. Had such a war crimes trial been carried out in Dhaka, not just that country but the entire global community would have understood the depths of depravity plumbed by the Pakistan Army in its genocide of East Bengalis.

These days, given the implicit security relationship between Islamabad and Beijing, concretized via the China Pakistan Economic Corridor (CPEC) agreement, there has been some

shedding by the Modi government of the earlier Indian
ambivalence. This has partly been achieved through deeper
involvement with Japan, the US and Australia, the three other
countries that are part of the Quad. However, unlike in the case
of the sudden leap represented by the Indo-Soviet treaty, the
operationalization of the Quad has proceeded at a creeping
pace, not least because of the traditional approach of the post-
1947 Lutyens Zone, which is (if we were to use a term common
in social discourse) to be 'willing to have a relationship but
not ready to commit'. Fortunately for India, during the PLA
intrusions that led to deadly clashes on the Sino-Indian border
in 2020, even though there was no formal 'commitment', the
US at least verbally (and almost certainly in more substantive
ways) backed India. Had there been a deeper level of strategic
understanding between Washington and Delhi (something that
has remained anathema to those policymakers in both capitals
who are steeped in Cold War 1.0 logic that sees Delhi as being
linked at the hip with Moscow), there could have been a seamless
flow of supplies between the US and India since 2017. It needs
remembering that the period from 2017 saw a recurrence of the
active phase of the Sino-Indian border conflict, underlining the
need for a steady flow of supplies and assistance to India as the
country faced the principal adversary of the democracies in the
era of Cold War 2.0.

Such supplies would have added to the existing professional
skills and readiness for battle of the Indian Armed Forces to
ensure not simply the blocking of further expansion into
Indian territory by the PLA, but the recovery by the Indian
Armed Forces of some of the territory lost since 1947. Such
an 'offensive' strategy appears to remain beyond the ambit of
options considered by the politicians and civilian officials who
continue to micromanage the military establishment in India

even during periods of war. A silver lining is that the position of chief of defence staff (CDS) caused by the passing away of Bipin Rawat in December 2021 has been continued rather than abandoned. It is expected of the new CDS General Chauhan that he will as secretary to the government emulate the example of his specialist peers in the atomic energy and space ministries. The space and atomic programmes have made remarkable progress despite comprehensive sanctions against India, in a manner that departments headed by generalist administrators have failed to do. As a domain specialist, General Chauhan needs to imprint his views on the policy recommendations made or forwarded to the cabinet committee on security, rather than defer to generalist administrators as was the case previous to the CDS appointment.

In the name of 'Strategic Ambiguity' or more grandly, 'Strategic Autonomy' what has long been carried out in practice is the long-standing pseudo-stratagem of Strategic Ambivalence.[2] An example is policy towards the Russian Federation. 'Autonomy' or 'Ambiguity' is sought to be maintained by purchasing from Russia weapons critical in conflict situations, even as purchases from the US grow. This is caused by the placing of weapons purchases in separate military and financial silos, in the process not taking into account the differential geopolitical impact of the purchase, installation and use of US and Russian systems. Going forward with purchasing naval vessels (including undersea craft) from Russia would not present problems of coordination of activities with Quad navies, despite the absence of such vessels in their respective fleets. Nor would the purchase of aircraft. However, keeping in view the

---

[2] M.D. Nalapat, 'Ambivalence Is Neither Strategic Ambiguity Nor Autonomy', *Sunday Guardian*, April 3, 2021, https://www.sundayguardianlive.com/opinion/ambivalence-neither-strategic-ambiguity-autonomy.

ever-closer coordination between the Chinese and Russian militaries, an assumption needs to be made that supplies from Moscow may get impacted were there to be an intensification of kinetic actions between India and China.

A helpful move would be for the naval and air platforms to be made within India, something that Moscow had been very cooperative in facilitating during the days of the Soviet Union, but much less so since the implosion of the USSR. Ideally, India needs to be a production base for not just domestically made systems, but to manufacture systems sourced from allies such as the US. The latter would find such outsourcing helpful as well, in that it would cut costs and improve competitive capability of such systems against competition from other sources. However, it is clear that the trajectory of the Sino-Russian alliance is making it desirable that India decouple itself from Russian defence systems, although continuing to buy oil and other resources from that long-standing partner (Russia).

The US administration under Biden appears to have taken a pragmatic decision to not be in a rush to impose CAATSA (Countering America's Adversaries Through Sanctions Act) sanctions on India consequent to the purchase by Delhi of five S-400 missile defence systems from Russia. This has led to much congratulatory backslapping in the Lutyens Zone, but such elation sidesteps the problem that continued purchase of Russian-made defence equipment pushes further into the future the issue of reducing and finally eliminating reliance on Russian defence platforms. Such a shift is warranted in view of the ties that have been established between the PRC and Russian Federation defence and security establishments. Leaving the safety of India to trust in Russia not sharing critical information with China where the defence systems it supplies to India are concerned may not be the optimal manner of dealing with the country's defence and security.

Even if the S-400 systems supplied to India are not embedded with PRC components as feared by some experts in the field, the fact remains that technicians and others from the Russian Federation may need to be intensively involved in the setting up and maintenance of this system in India, possibly in sensitive locations. Given the increasing degree of fit between the Russian and Chinese defence and security establishments, it would be difficult to aver with full confidence that an exchange of information about the Indian Armed Forces is not taking place between the military establishments of the two partners in the Sino-Russian alliance. Such an information flow may include information on the potency (and how to dilute this) of at least some of the Russian military platforms supplied to India. The S-400 has the capability to map several of the performance parameters of aircraft operating within the range of its scopes and may transmit such data not necessarily only to the Indian buyers but to the Russian suppliers, and through them possibly to agencies interested in such information within the PRC, including within the PLA.

Placing reliance on defence requisites against the armed forces of a country on another country that is the closest military partner of one's principal foe may not be a prudent course to follow. Relying on Russia for military preparedness against China is to rely on a country that has the closest coordination with the 'threat' country in matters of defence and intelligence. The installation of S-400 would result in a substantial increase in the existing subliminal level of mistrust between Cold War 1.0 elements, in particular between Washington and Delhi, in that the purchase and installation would continue for almost a generation more of heavy reliance of the Indian Armed Forces on Russian equipment. It has the consequent potential to result in a significant dilution of the lethal assistance needed to be provided to the Indian Armed Forces by the US. This would be designed to deal with any intensification of the ongoing conflict with China, out of worry that the performance capabilities of such equipment may get mapped by Russian systems active in India, or Chinese systems such as drones that continue to remain in use within India. Rather than having gone forward with operationalizing S-400 systems in India, it would have been better to use the option to negotiate with Washington so as to get installed (at a steeply discounted cost reflecting the gain to US security of such a system being installed in India and forming part of the Quad architecture of mutual defence) Terminal High Altitude Area Defence (THAAD) systems in India. At the same time, the money committed towards the purchase of the five S-400 systems could have been rerouted towards the purchase of other items from the Russian Federation, such as oil and gas assets. Vigorous action on the proposal for a Vladivostok-Chennai Maritime Corridor could financially compensate Moscow for the decline in weapons purchases needed as a consequence of the coming together of Beijing and Moscow in a comprehensive strategic alliance with a strong military and technological component. Russia has been and should remain an essential partner of India in trade volume, but no longer in the field of provision of defence items that could make the difference between success and failure in a kinetic conflict between China and India. Once having signed on to the Quad, there is a certain logic to events that needs to be accepted and followed, not denied in practice, if the joint objective of a free and open Indo-Pacific is to be met.

Any worsening of relations between the US and Russia (or India) suits the interests of China. Throughout the Ukraine conflict, Xi's interest has been to ensure that Russia remain in the conflict, no matter how many times Beijing's protestations of seeking a 'peaceful settlement' get repeated. At the same time, it can offer its services as a presumed honest broker between the Atlantic Alliance and Russia, similar to the manner in which the PRC is seeking to mediate between India and Pakistan. In the Ukraine war, the PRC interest is to ensure that Russia continues to fight well into 2023, so that relations between Moscow and the Atlantic Alliance worsen, increasing a mood of accommodation within the Atlantic Alliance towards China. In the India-Pakistan situation, it has been clear from the 1960s that the preferred side of Beijing is Islamabad (or more accurately, Rawalpindi) and not Delhi. Offers of mediation are simply PRC's means to gain leverage and promote its interests as determined by the CPC leadership.

The Cold War 1.0 mindset that remains abundant within the US Congress and the administration prevents them from drawing necessary conclusions and arriving at the fact that the worse ties between Russia and the EU get, the better for China. The more isolated Moscow is, the greater will be its dependence on Beijing. And given the undesirability of a two-front war involving both China and Russia, the worse relations with Moscow get, the greater will be the impetus for the NATO powers to attempt an accommodation with China, to the benefit of the latter as Xi continues his expansionary, aggressive path and begins to materialize some of his threats. In the Ukraine conflict, it must be admitted that Prime Minister Modi's refusal to follow the NATO line of all-out condemnation of Russia was not Strategic Ambiguity but, in this case, at least Strategic Clarity. The manner in which NATO has responded to the conflict merely plays into the hands of the PRC by diverting attention away from China to Russia, and from the Indo-Pacific back to the Atlantic, as was the case during the 1939–45 war between the Allies and the Axis and the period of Cold War 1.0 between the USSR and the US.

A policy of Strategic Autonomy needs to entail India substituting its defence relationship with a comprehensive economic partnership with Russia, which would benefit both countries substantially in a manner that would not affect the most significant security relationships they have with other countries. In Russia's case, this is with China, something that President Putin is unambiguous about directly and through Foreign Minister Sergey Lavrov, although the same degree of clarity is often not shown by their counterparts in Beijing. In India's case, the principal relationship needs to be with the US. Until now, the ideological haze surrounding the Lutyens Zone has prevented several of the voices favouring such a pairing from expressing this out loud. Where an economic linkage with Russia is concerned, the Vladivostok-Chennai Sea corridor would be a valuable segment of Russia-India cooperation, and could be implemented in tandem with Japan, should Tokyo and Moscow escape from their mutual antipathy towards each other.

Given the influx of settlers from the PRC into several parts of the Russian Federation, a similar influx from India would assist in ensuring an absence of success at any effort by Beijing at 'remote control' of parts of daily life in such regions through settlers from the PRC. In contrast to those entering from the PRC, settlers from India would be entirely free of attached geopolitical strings, except of course their welcome desire that Moscow and Delhi remain close to each other in the manner that they have been since the 1960s. There are numerous fields where India and Russia could collaborate without degrading the security of either the US or China respectively in any manner.

Of course, such a coming together of two future superpowers may impact efforts by Washington and Beijing to exercise a higher degree of control over policy in India and the Russian Federation, respectively. This would be a plus in the context of the need to retain 'Strategic Autonomy' by Russia as well as India. Such Indo-Russian collaboration would coexist together with the existing visible and implied alliance mechanisms of Moscow and Delhi. The Kremlin would thereby get the breathing space needed to move away at least partially from PRC-suggested measures designed to subserve not Moscow's interests but those of Beijing.

The CPC relies on the chequebook as an important facilitator of its policies, besides of course the military, the second of which has come to the fore since Xi assumed charge in 2012. Rather than seek to compete with China in that game, India needs to leverage its people-to-people, cultural and commercial strengths, including ensuring good relations with Russia, a country that has established its value as a partner across several decades. President Putin would welcome for himself and the country he leads the freedom to act in a manner that safeguards and promotes the Russian interest rather than merely be a force multiplier for the expansionist agenda of CPC General Secretary Xi. Neither the US nor the PRC would be pleased at an increase in warmth between India and Russia, but such a pairing carried forward in a calibrated and suitable manner would serve the interests of both the Indian as well as the Russian people without putting at risk the significant relationship that exists between the two and Washington and Beijing, respectively.

Not searching more intensively for payment options when confronted with Trump-era financial sanctions on Iran out of worry for the economic consequences of such sanctions, while simultaneously going forward with the purchase of S-400 systems that opened the door to CAATSA sanctions by the Biden administration, represents another of the numerous examples of policies that were framed in a context where the reality of Cold War 2.0 was ignored. This may have been in the fact that an embrace of such potentially sub-primal options has been the bedrock of the doctrine of Strategic Ambiguity, not to mention 'autonomy'. Of course, in some cases such actions merely arise out of confusion and absence of clarity in judging outcomes, traits that have long accompanied the practice of 'Strategic Ambivalence' followed within the Lutyens Zone. Ancient wisdom in India holds that 'it is better to aim at the stars and miss rather than aim at the moon and hit'. Policymakers steeped in the traditions developed over the decades since the 1950s of the Lutyens Zone aim at neither the stars nor the moon, but at nearby mounds of earth, and sometimes end up missing even that. The good news for them is that the fog of misinformation that blankets so much commentary in India provides a suitable medium to transform failure into success through spin and the release of titbits of (sometimes erroneous) information designed to promote belief in what the officials claim is the sole truth.

Spin it any way, Iran is an essential partner of India, and it was an error to have acted in a manner during the Trump administration that put at risk the long-term interests of not just India but ultimately the US as well. For Washington would benefit were India, now among its most important partners, to retain a good relationship with Iran, a country too significant within the environs of the Middle East to exclude. This lesson appears to have been learnt by Saudi Arabia and the UAE, although it has been for long standard practice in Qatar, among the canniest of the Gulf Cooperation Council (GCC) states. The perception of unreliability in the face of US pressure that was exhibited by India in its role of a long-time buyer of Iranian crude during the period when President Trump imposed sanctions on Iran weakened Tehran's trust in the staying power and therefore the reliability in a crisis of India, and propelled Tehran towards further movement into the Chinese orbit.

Fortunately, being a country that values its own Strategic Autonomy, Iran has retained its close linkages with India, a factor that is important when the Chabahar project enters the equation. This project would ensure a route separate from that available (but not yet to India) through the PRC's client, Pakistan. Chabahar provides an alternative route that could in time be used by the other Quad members to trade with Central Asia and Afghanistan. The PRC, by its refusal to go by US sanctions against Tehran during the Trump presidency, has secured the upper hand over India in its relationship with Iran.[3] However, the manner in which Beijing seeks to assertively promote its agenda in every country, and the manner in which PRC commercial entities seek to generate immediate benefits from any country that they are active in, may give pause to Tehran, should India prove itself in future to be a reliable option.

Despite occasional vacillations caused by the contortions of the policy of Strategic Ambivalence exhibited by policymakers within the Lutyens Zone, a close relationship with India confers several advantages for Iran. In particular, those ruling the country are aware of the fact that the Shia community in Pakistan suffers from under-representation (especially in the military and in business) and repression, and that GHQ Rawalpindi has for decades provided assistance to separatist Wahhabi groups

---

[3] 'China's Budding Relationship with Iran Is a Threat to India', *The Hindu Business Line*, July 19, 2020, https://www.thehindubusinessline.com/opinion/editorial/chinas-budding-relationship-with-iran-is-a-threat-to-india/article32131468.ece.

operating in Iran, in large part to please Washington. For Iran, Pakistan is unreliable structurally, no matter what Islamabad's public promises of friendship may be. Which may explain the lack of success thus far in Beijing's bid to get Iran to join hands with Islamabad in asymmetric operations that concern India.

Supreme leader of Iran Ayatollah Ruhollah Khomeini, who spent much of his life 'learning by contemplation and experience' in a seminary in Qom, believed that strident championing of the Palestinian cause and denunciation of Israel would assure Iran the goodwill of Muslims worldwide. His other axiom was that the only way to so champion the Palestinian cause was to be a votary of the Single State solution, wherein the State of Israel would be made to disappear from the map. The 'Zionist entity' would be replaced by an Islamic Republic of Palestine mentored by the supreme leader of Iran. While much of Khomeini's vituperation against Israel was verbal, there began a process of support for Palestinian and other groups that were and still remain engaged in armed struggle with the Jewish state. In this, Iran was only doing what several Arab and other states were doing. The difference was that in their case, it was 'private' citizens and 'non-governmental' organizations which took up the funding, equipping and training of groups engaged in acts of violence against the State of Israel. In the case of Iran, the clerical regime was more transparent than the regime elements in some Arab states that were in direct involvement in such activities. Added to the anger against the Iranian regime in the US generated by the embassy hostage crisis of 1979–80 was the build-up of similar views about post-1979 Iran among decision-makers in Israel and the initiation of countermeasures against the Islamic Republic of Iran, steps which continue to this day. Hardly a surprise, given the widespread dissemination of slogans proclaiming that the clerical regime's goal is 'Death to America', accompanied by 'Death to the Zionist Entity (Israel)'.

The reaction of Israel and its friends to such activities by Iran was a boon to Saudi Arabia in particular, which was wary of the efforts being made by Iran to displace it as the fulcrum of influence in the Muslim populations of the world. This was never a realistic possibility, given the fact that the Shia component of the global Muslim population comprises barely 15 per cent of the total, plus the economic under-performance of Iran as a consequence of sanctions imposed as a consequence of activities hostile to Israel as well as to the perpetuation of Washington's influence in the Middle East. Apart from its frayed relations with the US and mutual hostility with Israel, Tehran has had to contend with the systematic campaign led by Saudi Arabia to undercut its influence in the region.

It is this phalanx of states—that are active in opposition to Iran—that offer an opportunity for India to establish deeper ties with that very consequential country in a manner that would not cause damage to Delhi's ties with the countries opposed to Iran, such as the US, Israel and Saudi Arabia, all of which are important in sustaining India's trajectory towards the aspiration of becoming the world's third superpower. During Cold War 1.0 there were only two such behemoths, and this far, this is the case in Cold War 2.0, with the PRC having replaced the USSR as the alternative superpower to the US. By now, India ought to have been the third member of that club, but for policy missteps that have been made since the 1950s within the Lutyens Zone. Iran is important to India not merely as a supplier of crude or culturally, but because of its value as a land bridge to Central Asia and Afghanistan in a situation where access by and to India has been blocked by Pakistan in another of the ultimately self-defeating measures in GHQ Rawalpindi's anti-India basket.

In the Middle East and in Southeast Asia, long-standing cultural and historical linkages combine with present India as a more attractive alternative to either the authoritarian structure represented by the PRC, or the religious extremism and exclusivism that has been in vogue in Pakistan and in some other countries. The imperative of progress in the twenty-first century mandates a freedom of thought and belief as well as lifestyle, and sometimes through legislation, other times through judicial orders, such a situation has been gathering pace in India as well. This is less the creation of the government than the empowerment of the individual through the information and freedom of action made available by information technology, factors that will gather speed once 5G comes into widespread operation in India.

From the manner in which tariff policy was tweaked by Finance Minister Manmohan Singh in the 1990s to facilitate the dumping of computer hardware into India rather than his government building up national champions, domestic technology and entrepreneurship—not to mention the Indian rupee—have long been treated in a stepmotherly fashion when contrasted with the red carpet extended to foreign enterprises. For around fifteen years, much of this has come from the PRC, the country that is the force multiplier and facilitator for GHQ Rawalpindi in the latter's operations against India. Talent from India has had to migrate to other countries or work in foreign companies because of the absence of support they have long been getting from the governmental mechanism in India, a situation that is finally being remedied under Modi 2.0. Tech companies that are shut out of business in India owing to implicit and invisible preferences that in the past were given to foreign enterprises often go abroad and service the very countries and companies that export products and processes to India.

Foreign companies are welcome to set up production facilities in India, except that those linked to countries that are hostile to India need to be prevented from accessing the domestic market, especially in fields that could be of value to their military and cyber operations against the world's most populous democracy. That even companies majorly operating in Pakistan-occupied Kashmir are not, as a consequence, barred from doing any business in India is indicative of the effects of ambivalence as the driving force of so much policy. It is telling that branches in Pakistan of international companies felt no resistance in sending tweets dismissive of Indian security concerns while the branches in India of the same companies have refrained from similar abuse of Pakistan.

India has edged closer to the US, a situation created in part as the result of the actions of the Sino-Pakistan duo but overall, as a consequence of the confluence of interests of the two biggest democracies. Israel too is an important partner, as is the UAE. Prime Minister Modi will need to convince Jerusalem and Washington that it is in the fundamental interests of both the US as well as Israel that a friend and de facto ally (India) retain a relationship of trust with Iran that may be of value in a future contingency. An example of such value was the effort in 2012 by officials linked to the Assad government in Damascus to convey via a strategic analyst in India that they were open to settling outstanding disputes with Israel. The Alawite community, to which former Syrian President Bashar Assad belongs, is known for its modernity and moderation, which is why it is a particular target of armed Wahhabi groups that have been active in Syria through the patronage of countries seeking to depose Assad in the manner that they did Muammar Gaddafi, a Libyan politician, in 2011. Both Washington (at that time under the Obama administration) and Jerusalem were adamant during that time (2012) that Bashar Assad would go the way of Gaddafi that year itself. An opportunity of making a peace that may have shut the Syrian gateway for the flow of external assistance to anti-Israel groups in Palestine was lost. Even the First Lady Asma Assad in Damascus had publicly received the offer of a comfortable asylum in Europe with her family, with the condition that she abandon her husband, President Bashar Assad to his fate. To Asma Assad's credit, the offer was treated with the contempt that it merited. It is now 2023 and not only is Bashar Assad still holding sway in Damascus but he has strengthened his position in terms of control of territory since the time when informal feelers were made by influential Syrian officials about the possibility of negotiating a reconciliation with Israel.

At that point in time, it was likely that Iran too would have agreed to an understanding that was much more generous to the other side than its negotiating position that prevailed until the 2011 unrest in Syria. That opportunity for a settlement with Syria was never seized, in the belief that the Assad regime in Damascus as well as the clerical regime in Tehran would collapse as a consequence of public unrest caused by conflict and economic distress. It may be added that Israeli Prime Minister Benjamin Netanyahu was subsequently able to declare sovereignty over the entire Golan Heights in 2019, a move legitimized by the Trump administration, whereas any negotiation with the Assad government in 2012–13 would have almost certainly ended in only a partial establishment of legal control over the Golan Heights and its waters, which meet a third of Israel's needs. However, the flow via Syria from outside powers of assistance to groups hostile to Israel in the Palestinian territories (including Gaza) and Lebanon continues.

Although as President of the United States, Trump was responsible for some major missteps in foreign and security policy, among his achievements was the normalization of relations between important Middle Eastern states such as the UAE and Israel, the same way as the 1978 Camp David accords were between third Egyptian President Anwar Sadat and sixth Israeli Prime Minister Menachem Begin, followed by a similar warming of ties with the Hashemite kingdom of Jordan. Both these initial accords have endured, and the 2020 accords between Israel and Morocco, Bahrain, Sudan and the UAE are likely to as well. In none of this was India involved, despite requests in the past from some of the players in the Middle East that the world's largest democracy try its hand at efforts promoting normalization between Israel and GCC states. In large part, this is because of the long-standing fixation within the Lutyens Zone with the Palestine issue, and the accompanying implicit assumption that this needs to be out of the way before other peace and normalization options get explored. President Trump disagreed that the entire process of Arab-Israeli normalization had to await a 'mutually satisfactory' resolution of the Palestine problem. Interestingly, such an assumption is very similar to that of the Government of Pakistan in negotiations with India, that unless the 'Kashmir issue' gets resolved in a manner favourable to GHQ Rawalpindi, other processes of normalization would either proceed only at a crawl or not at all. However, none of this dilutes the desirability of India being a safety valve to the US where Iran is concerned, such as through facilitating the movement of goods from the US to Afghanistan via Iran. This assumes salience because the re-establishing of the Taliban as the fount of authority in Kabul, as promoted by Pakistan aided by China, is as little in the interests of Tehran as it is for Delhi. Gestures that resemble salami slicing more than anything else are insufficient to build the stable and operationally significant relationships that India would be best served by, but the vacillations caused by the policy of Strategic Ambivalence followed by India have made this difficult.

Unlike the situation in the US, that other member of the 'Big Two' of the democratic world, the foreign policy of India continues to be a 'closed shop' that comprises officials who reached their positions after, in their youth, getting through an examination system similar to the one that began in Imperial China during the Sui dynasty, which was established in 581 and lasted until AD 618. Favoured think tanks have traditionally been encouraged not to offer contrarian views but to present justifications for policies favoured within the portals of the external affairs ministry and the Prime Minister's Office. Such a mechanism places a high degree of relevance form in place of outcome. An example of the effects of choosing to form over substance was the protocol situation that prevailed soon after the 1979 takeover by Khomeini of power in Iran. Clerics became the arbiters of policy rather than the government headed by Abolhassan Banisadr, with some playing an outsized role in the determination of policy. Although first Iranian President Seyyed Abolhassan Banisadr and others such as Sadegh Ghotbzadeh, a close aide of Khomeini, sought to limit the powers over governance of the clerics, they were tossed aside (Banisadr escaped to exile while Ghotbzadeh was executed in 1982). Either unaware of the state of power dynamics in Tehran or out of a reflexive adherence to the compulsions of formal protocol, even a deputy minister or other senior officials in the hierarchy of the (in several respects, powerless) Iranian government was given VVIP treatment on arrival to India. In contrast, even the more influential of clerics (unless they were simultaneously holding an official position) visiting India were given the usual treatment meted out to mere members of civil society from the time of their arrival to India. This could not have assisted in endearing India to them. Another example of fealty to form over substance was the choice of the chief guest at the 2019 Republic Day parade. Reports were that President Trump had declined the honour (most likely because he had an allergy to following in the path of President Obama who had been the chief guest in 2015). Indications from Washington were that Vice-President Mike Pence would have been happy to come instead, but this move got zero traction in the Lutyens Zone, as a mere vice-president was no substitute for a president, who duly arrived in the persona of Cyril Ramaphosa of South Africa. Given that Pence, who till January 2021 had substantial traction within the White House, could have been persuaded to fast-track and to develop initiatives from the US government side that would have been of mutual benefit, his choice as guest of honour at the 2019 Republic Day parade would have had the potential of being much more valuable to overall Indian interests than the admittedly distinguished and capable South African president. But in the Lutyens Zone, titles count, and that of President naturally carries more weight than that of vice-president, even of the US.

The speed of development of technology has resulted in the twenty-first century becoming distinguished by a 'horizontalization' of perceptions about different societies. This is different from the 'vertical' (or hierarchical) model that had been followed until then. In this schema, certain societies were regarded as being on a more elevated level than others. The development of technology has enabled the dissemination of knowledge and opportunity to a larger and larger proportion of the population of the globe. Within countries, there is enhanced interest in, and discovery of, traditions which go back into history. Hence the spread within the US of uniquely 'African American' names in place of the standard names common to the largest segment of the population in the US, those of European descent. In the US, fringe groups with indirect (and often unknown to participants) linkages to China and Russia, the PRC's biggest ally, infiltrated both 'Left' movements such as Black Lives Matter as well as 'Right' groups such as those within the mobs that marched on the US Capitol on 6 January 2021. They indulged in violence that had the effect of de-legitimizing the cause to which they claimed to be committed. However, such aberrations do not obscure the fact that it is no longer acceptable to look askance on specific cultures, especially those derived from societies that were the victims of the slave trade (as in the case of those transported to the US from Africa) or mass murder (as with the Incas by the Spaniards). Both in Africa as well as in South America the vibrant culture and lifestyles of ancient times are being rediscovered with a new-found pride in such an ancestry. It needs to be added that several such recoveries of ancient cultural ways and treasures have been the result of research by those of European descent, and many in that ethnic group have joined the ranks of those who are celebrating and showcasing newly discovered knowledge of the vibrancy of the past of societies that were overrun and, in some instances, extinguished by colonial expansion and depredation.

As in the African continent, the people of South America are going through such a process. Among the consequences has been the coming to power of politicians outside those who are (wholly or mostly) of European origin, and who have long been in authority in many of the countries of the continent. India has the potential of being the beneficiary of such a change in terms of diplomatic closeness and geopolitical salience. The country has since 1947 instituted affirmative action on a scale not seen even in South Africa after the ascension to the presidency of Nelson Mandela in 1994. However, the essentially defensive and reactive approach to international policy of India had prevented the tapping of the rich vein of interest in the world's oldest democracy with several of its cultural traditions going back as much as six millennia. Another inhibiting factor was the persistence of colonial teachings that classify much of the ancient history of India as being 'unproven', and therefore it was dismissed as myth. Marrying culture with diplomacy as well as a comprehensive review of history has been the practice since Narendra Modi took over as prime minister in 2014. Six years later, a New Education Policy was unveiled that was designed to substantially rectify such defects in the colonial-era teaching of the culture, traditions and history of India. The present prime minister has also initiated an Act East policy that builds on the foundation of ancient cultural and trade links between India and the countries of Southeast Asia.

A similar alacrity of development of relationships needs to take place in Africa and in South America. In the latter continent, far from seeking to capitalize on the growing pride in past traditions of the people, a leader who is a poster boy for the disappearing era of domination of the Europeanized elements of the population of the continent was invited as the guest of honour at the 2020 Republic Day parade on Rajpath. The divergence between the 'vertical' practices and policies of President Jair Bolsonaro of Brazil and the 'horizontal' precepts that Prime Minister Modi of India holds dear, especially in relation to its own people, was ignored as a consequence of the obsessive respect for form in the taking of such decisions within the Lutyens Zone. The fact is that Bolsonaro, even though he was President of Brazil, was a throwback to an earlier era rather than the tribune of a new era as (thirty-fifth) President Luiz Inacio da Silva was in the past and has once again emerged. The time may have come for a transformational ex-president or non-president to be invited as chief guest for the Republic Day parade on Rajpath. The time is awaited when a fighter for human rights or a great littérateur will be the guest of honour at the Republic Day parade on Rajpath, rather than only individuals with impressive formal titles.

Ambivalence in the guise of autonomy has prevented India from leveraging its cultural and historical strengths to strike deep chords within the awakening of traditional culture in much of South America. Given the colonial complex that suffuses the functioning of the bureaucracy, as well as a reflexive inferiority complex born out of centuries of humiliation at the hands of external conquerors, it is perhaps no surprise that so much Indian diplomacy in South America has gravitated towards the Euro-ethnic segment rather than the indigenous. The lavishing of attention on Jair Bolsonaro was an example of such a course of action. Far better would have been a systematic campaign throughout the continent to link up with, and show support and empathy for, efforts at retrieving and reviving its ancient pre-colonization heritage. Of course, this needs to be in a manner reflective of the values of Mahatma Gandhi or Nelson Mandela rather than the vindictive streak witnessed during the rule in Zimbabwe of Robert Mugabe. The prejudice inherent in racism is evil, whether it be of one form or the other. The India story is compelling for so many in Africa and South America.

Since Modi became prime minister in 2014, he has presided over an immense effort at rediscovering India's past and celebrating it rather than ignoring it. In every country where there is a significant population of those who trace their ethnicity to India, at least a few individuals are trusted by top policymakers as friends or advisers on some matter or the other. What is required is a far more comprehensive scan of such individuals, so that through visits to India and meetings with key policymakers they may be made aware of the appreciation that their ancestral home has for their achievements. NGOs are important vessels of influence, and whether it be the PRC or the Atlantic Alliance, these have frequently been (sometimes unwittingly) pressed into service to serve goals set by the government of the country they are headquartered in while claiming otherwise.

The linking of the word 'nationalist' with a religious tag is a contradiction in terms. International media outlets frequently use the term 'Hindu nationalists'. Usually, if this refers to those considered 'nationalist' who also subscribe to the Hindu faith, the term 'Hindu' is superfluous. Is Boris Johnson an Anglican or a British nationalist? Is Emmanuel Macron a Catholic nationalist or a French nationalist? The term 'Hindu nationalist' is narrowly used by some to refer to those few who regard only those belonging to the Hindu faith as being legitimately Indian. The roots of such a view are usually a reaction to the period preceding the 1947 partition of the country on the absurd basis that Hindus and Muslims form 'two nations'. In Pakistan, non-Muslims have been nearly eliminated since 1947, but it is nonsense to claim that a similar demographic alteration needs to take place in India as well. Or indeed that Pakistan has gained rather than lost (as it has) from becoming an almost mono-religious country. The squeezing out of the Hindu, Sikh and Christian minorities in Pakistan is an unconscionable act not mitigated by the almost complete silence of self-proclaimed global champions of human rights about such an outcome, and ought not to be copied by any civilized nation, least of all a country that has as its bedrock belief the concept of Sanatan Dharma, the acceptance of multiple paths towards the attainment of union with eternity.

Catching a trend in its very early days and riding on it to success needs to be an important component of Smart Policy. In the case of anti-colonial struggle waged by India, although it unfortunately ended in the bitterness of Partition, ensured that in India, similar struggles in other parts of the world were treated sympathetically. This was a correct policy, although some of the tactics and messaging used during the 1950s and 1960s may be questioned. An example from 2021 of how a trend towards free elections and responsible governments was ignored in favour of the usual ambivalence was the subdued response of Delhi on the 1 February 2021 military coup in Myanmar. It was obvious that the people of the country would not acquiesce in such a repeat of the past half-century of such rule, just as the people of Afghanistan will decline not just the overlordship (as during 1996–2001) of the Taliban but the restrictive policies that are being reintroduced by that regressive entity once NATO allowed it to control the central government in Kabul. While avoiding the sanctions morass, a less ambivalent policy towards the illegal takeover of power from an elected government headed by Aung San Suu Kyi was best from the viewpoint of longer-term interests. The manner in which the coup was reacted to by Delhi was certainly not 'ambiguous', especially when India joined the PRC, Russia and Pakistan in being represented at that year's Army Day parade in the capital of Myanmar rather than staying away, as the world's most populous democracy ought to have. A return to civilian rule under the leader chosen by the people of Myanmar is inevitable, and such a government once formed will not forget India and its ambivalence during Myanmar's coup-induced travail. A major power, not to mention an aspiring superpower, needs to speak and conduct itself in a clear rather than confusing manner where fundamental precepts are concerned. Looking at the mishmash of mutually contradictory policies that Strategic Ambivalence has resulted in where India is concerned, it is evident that substantial changes need to be made about the very approach to policy formulation. There needs to be no ambiguity about this in a country where the governance system has long made a fetish out of what it considers a virtue, which is to avoid taking sides even when it is imperative to do so.

5

Self-Goals Cause Europe's
Steady Decline

Although there has long been a conceptual separation of Europe from Asia, in geopolitical terms, the line starting from the Arctic, moving across the Ural Mountains, and finally meandering down into the Mediterranean is arbitrary. This will be disputed by those who point to (what they believe to be) significant differences in the populations of both, which for an extended historical epoch was defined in terms of skin colour, with the 'white' population living in Europe and those of other hues in Asia. Theories of racial exclusivism and superiority continue to be expressed, although not as commonly as in the past. The pseudo-science that was a characteristic of the belief system of the NSDAP postulated a 'pure Aryan race', neglecting the settlement over centuries of migrants from the southern and eastern portions of Europe. Or the impact on the genetic composition of the German population from the fact that much of the territory which they inhabited had been in the path of Mongol conquests, and that several of the conquerors settled down with local women and bred families that swiftly got dissolved into the rest of the population. There are indeed broad classifications of ethnicities, but the word 'purity' (referring to complete insularity of breeding) is out of place in any fact-based analysis of the issue, apart from being a genetic disaster. There have indeed been small communities of individuals who have through isolation avoided any mingling from the outside, but none of these have been distinguished for any hint of excellence in human endeavour. Indeed, an incontrovertible case could be made that ethnic diversity promotes excellence far more than exclusion. In Germany under the Nazis, the persecution and elimination of the Jewish community deprived Hitler's war machine of some of the most talented minds in the country, including so far as carrying forward the science of weaponry was concerned. It cannot be forgotten that the atom bomb was developed in the US principally by Jewish scientists who had fled Germany and other parts of Europe to escape persecution and annihilation. Others who stayed behind were dealt with in the genocidal manner capsuled as the 'Final Solution to the Jewish Problem'. The lack of science and reason, not to mention common humanity, of the Nazi movement prevented Hitler and his accomplices from understanding that their 'Final Solution' brought closer the defeat of Germany in World War II by eliminating some of the most talented individuals in the state. The killing of members of the Jewish community in the Holocaust was a global catastrophe. This single action aborted countless discoveries in science, literature and other fields of learning that those who perished in the gas chambers would have been the creators of, had they continued their lives and work. If in the past, it was Genghis Khan who was a global object of horror, from the 1940s that role has been taken by Hitler.

Self-destructive policies by the leading powers of Europe are what led to the downfall of their dominance in Asia, Africa and South America. World War I weakened the participating European colonial states so much that it made the independence of colonies in Asia inevitable. Freedom movements in different countries adopted divergent methods of securing the independence from European control that they sensed to be within reach. India, Indonesia and Vietnam saw divergent paths, with the latter two countries managing to retain their unity at the conclusion of the process of decolonization, while India was partitioned on the senseless basis of religion. While Mahatma Gandhi shared the secular vision of Subhas Chandra Bose in looking at Hindus and Muslims as parts of a united people, in contrast to the former, the latter was more successful in bringing the different faiths together. This was within the Indian National Army, which Bose fashioned in his efforts at armed struggle against the British in India, a struggle assisted at that time by Japan. The Mahatma had less success. He could not prevent M.A. Jinnah from persuading a substantial chunk of the Indian Muslim community (ironically, as the boundaries of the two states turned out, in UP and Bihar far more than in Punjab and Sindh) that their future lay in separation from India and the formation of a country in which Muslims would dominate. The year 1975 saw the unification of Vietnam under the Communist Party, while in contrast 1947 witnessed the division of India. There was also a division, presumed at the time to be temporary, caused through errors in policy by the Nehru government. This was in the former princely state of Jammu and Kashmir. Freedom from control of colonized people by Europeans had become inevitable because of the enervation and social unrest in Europe that was caused by World War I. Independence began to become a reality in colony after colony soon after the close of World War II as a consequence of the weakening of European countries through the ravages of the war.

Apart from fighting two major internecine conflicts during the first half of the twentieth century, another self-goal by the European powers was to regard the populations of the territories colonized by them in a manner that failed to unlock their potential. They regarded it as axiomatic that such populations needed to be rendered incapable of matching the level of educational and other achievement of their conquerors. Severely discriminatory policies were introduced, which substantially resembled the policies later adopted by Nazi Germany when it occupied some countries in Europe, including those that had overseas colonies. The Nazis often treated other Europeans in the same manner as the latter treated the populations of the countries outside Europe that they colonized, although even as the Atlantic Charter was approved in 1941 by Prime Minister Winston Churchill of the United Kingdom and President Franklin Roosevelt of the United States, the former was insistent that the rights and freedoms mentioned in the charter should not apply to 'lesser races'.

In this matter, then United Kingdom Prime Minister Winston Churchill had views similar to those of the individual he abhorred, Hitler, and was not ashamed to proclaim his prejudices in private and public. Not a few others in his country shared the same views, which is why so many failed to comprehend the inhumanity in Hitler and sought to ensure peace by appeasing him. That is, until the actions by the German dictator reached such a level of aggression that war with his country and its Italian ally became inevitable. Had the people of India been given the same degree of freedom under the British Crown as citizens of Australia and Canada, the course of history may have been different during the era of Cold War 1.0 between the US and the USSR. However, those with a mindset that normalized racial discrimination would not consent to such a move, and the opportunity to establish a lasting long-term relationship between the UK and India as close as that between that country and Canada and Australia was lost in the 1930s. Had the populations of the countries that came under the sway of European powers been given access to education and opportunities, the resultant benefits would have accrued not just to them but to the countries that ruled them, had they adopted a policy based on the premise of a shared humanity. As the efforts of Big Pharma in the US and the EU to emasculate (through bans, sanctions and regulations) production of much cheaper and equally effective generic drugs in India demonstrate, the extractive Zero Sum policy that was among the most visible features of European colonialism continues to this day. Another example of how tenaciously old mindsets linger is the way in which former colonies in Asia, South America and Africa were sought in 2022 to be made to follow the instructions of their former colonial masters in the way such countries reacted to the Ukraine conflict.

European countries have historically been their own worst enemies, and this tendency is continuing even within the EU. An example is the manner in which that grouping has opposed efforts by the Catalan population to decide through a referendum whether to remain part of Spain or to form a separate Catalan state. Although some of the leaders who call for an independent Catalan state are opposed to the EU, such a stance has been caused less by fundamental differences with the concept of a broad unity within Europe as by the persistence of the hostile stance of EU headquarters in Brussels to any call for self-determination in Catalonia. The optimal solution would be for Catalonia to become independent of Spain, should that be the will of the majority of the Catalan population, and for both to remain within the EU. The freedom from the tyranny of frontiers that the EU gifted to its members until the unprecedented restrictions of the 'Covid Panic' that began in 2020 would have resulted in minimal disruption caused through such a division of the present Spanish state. In place of such a situation, what is in danger of taking place as a consequence of both the obstinacy of Madrid as well as Brussels to agree to self-determination is causing schisms in Catalonia that could have severe effects on law and order in the years to come.

In this, Spain needs to be contrasted with the UK, the government of which reacted in a very different way to the effort of Scottish nationalists to make that part of the kingdom separate and independent of London. Given the extra leeway that would be provided to Spanish nationals and interests in the event of a separation of Catalonia from the country through common EU membership, the visceral reaction of Madrid was unwarranted. After all, the main strength of the EU is the freedom of travel and work within the construct of its members. There are some states in Europe that would be better served by a division on the lines being suggested for Spain and Catalonia. An example is Bavaria and the rest of the Federal Republic of Germany. That state has long chafed while its distinctive character, traditions and practices are being overlaid, and in many ways overwhelmed, through its being part of the same country. A separation of Bavaria from Germany would cause very little disruption were both to remain within the EU, as ought to be the case. In the situation facing the UK as it deals with the demand for Scottish independence, a way out in the future could be for the UK prime minister to adopt the practical course and ensure that the borders of the UK remain open to Scotland, which in turn would join the EU and have open borders with the rest of its members. In much the same way, the borders of Northern Ireland could remain open to the rest of the UK, even while the borders of that province remain open to the Irish Republic. This would give the UK two freeways to the EU, even after its separation. The mechanism of that alliance forms a safety valve in the event of regional aspirations reaching levels that call for formal separation from the rest of the country, which is why it is inexplicable that such demands are fought rather than accepted in the interests of better all-round development of local traditions.

For long, the Franco-German axis held sway within the councils of the EU, given the ambivalence of the UK to the grouping even after having been made a member in 1973. It was this alliance that succeeded in ensuring the exclusion of the Russian Federation from the 'Common European Home' that Moscow had been anxious to join even during the Gorbachev years. Together, with assistance from the Clinton White House and subsequent Atlanticist-dominated US administrations, Berlin and Paris did not merely exclude the Russian Federation but sought together with the US and the UK to promote the steady descent of that country into global irrelevance. This was done through the expansion of NATO into countries bordering the Russian Federation and through sanctions designed to chain and dilute Russia's technological and economic progress. If a search were made for the 'root causes' of such a policy by the UK, US, France and Germany, they lie in the fact that the entry of the Russian Federation and the attendant benefits to that country of such an association would ensure that Moscow secure a position of influence within the EU and NATO second only to that of the US.

The ascent of Russia back to superpower status would commence in a manner that thus far has been stymied since the collapse of the USSR in 1991. Another reason may be somewhat more subterranean, and this involves ethnicity. The explicit operationalization of racism into Europe's policies when Adolf Hitler controlled state power in Germany made explicit racism less 'politically acceptable' subsequently in much of Europe. A perception of difference such as what made Churchill reluctant to extend the benefits promised by the Atlantic Alliance to populations not of European descent. Or the hyper-extractive and in several respects inhuman form of rule of Belgium over the Congo or the effort by the Dutch and the French to retake control of the colonies they had lost control of in Southeast Asia because of the military defeats suffered by them at the hands of Japan. A subterranean strain of racism persisted in some of the policies in more than a few European states. It needs to be said that such a tendency has been on the wane, largely due to a recognition of the essential common basis of humanity within the European populations. A 'vertical' (separate and unequal) conception of human society lingered long after Hitler was forced to commit suicide in a cellar in 1945. The entry of the Russian Federation into the EU or even as an ally would have, in the view of those opposed to this, instead converted the European continent into becoming the western segment of the Eurasian continent, in the manner that the Indian Ocean is the western part of the Indo-Pacific. Although the St Petersburg school swears by 'pure' European identity, Russia itself is a Eurasian rather than an entirely European country. The irony is that the Russian Federation would be empowered and not diminished through acceptance of the reality of it being a Eurasian rather than a European power. Despite the views of the St Petersburg 'Common European Home' school that President Putin leads is neither European nor Asian but the single largest buckle linking Asia and Europe into a single Eurasia.

In 1990, Chancellor Helmut Kohl of the Federal Republic of Germany (West Germany) ordered that East German currency would be accepted and replaced at the same parity by the West German currency Ostmark once the two segments had been unified. This ignored the much weaker status of the East German currency, and substantially boosted the costs of reconstruction. It made investment in what had been East Germany far less attractive than would have been the case had the value of the Ostmark been put at a level more closely reflecting the reality of the market. Although hailed for its generosity, in the medium term at least, Chancellor Kohl retarded the transformation of the east of the newly unified country. This was through raising the costs as a consequence of his ignoring the relative values of the East and West German currencies. To this day, the difference between 'West' and 'East' within Germany is palpable in a manner that need not have been.[1] The currency equalization was a self-goal by the largest economy within the EU. Part of the basis for Kohl's decision to equalize in exchange the West German and East German currencies was his belief that the German worker was intrinsically capable of working in a manner unique in the world, and as those from the east were of the same ethnicity, they would soon equalize productivity differences as well as work and other habits.

On an extended canvas, the EU has granted freedom of work and access to citizens of member states of the European Union while ensuring severe curbs on entry to those from Asia. An unschooled citizen of any EU member state has been free to live and work anywhere within that entity, but but a techie from Chennai or Hyderabad in India cannot do so, despite the latter having the potential to give much more

---

[1] 'How Divisions between East and West Germany Persist 30 Years after Reunification', The Conversation, November 9, 2019, https://theconversation. com/how-divisions-between-east-and-west-germany-persist-30-years-after-reunification-126297.

taxes to society in the EU countries. The system of basing the right of entry into the US for the work was altered to favour those (of whatever ethnicity) who had the experience and qualifications needed to be productive members of society, a reform that is an exception to several racially charged approaches adopted by some other countries and in a different era in the US or in Australia. Not approving of any immigrant (whatever the qualification or attributes) who was not of European ethnicity has been in essence at the heart of the immigration policy of the EU, although it must be added that several countries within that group are witnessing surges in migration, in some part because of errors committed by some members of the EU as well as the US in countries such as Libya, Afghanistan and Iraq. In 2022, another self-goal was scored, which was to move away from oil and gas from Russia, in the process sanctioning that country in a way that has caused shortages and inflation across much of the world, not excluding the members of NATO.

The 'Arab Spring' in the Middle East and North Africa and the 'Colour Revolutions' in some countries of East Europe were boosted by the support of US Secretary of State Hillary Rodham Clinton. With an understandable nostalgia for the period (1993–2001) that Bill Clinton was President of the US, the then secretary of state appears to have conflated street protests in such locations with those that took place during and after the collapse of the USSR. Unlike in the case of the movements in East Europe and in the former USSR that were essentially ideological in nature, those in the Middle East and North Africa were grounded in economic hardship, not in the hunger for democracy that Hillary Clinton, American journalist and diplomat Samantha Power and others prominent in the first term of President Obama thought was the defining motive of

those who poured on to streets in some Arab countries. Such
protesters were encouraged and multiplied by the policy of the
US government to dissuade authorities in the countries affected
from using what may be defined as the 'Standard Operating
Procedure' followed in the past by such authorities in similar
situations, which had been to quell such manifestations by
force. It had been pointed out by the present writer in 2011 itself
that the 'Arab Spring' was in danger of becoming a Wahhabi
Winter.[2] The cause of this was the fact that relatively small but
very well-organized and funded Wahhabi groups took over the
leadership of such popular manifestations, in much the same
manner as the expertly led and tightly organized Bolshevik
Party took charge of public resentment against the Kerensky
government for the then leader's fatal error of seeking to
prolong the war against Germany. By nudging Alexander
Kerensky into such a course of action, chancelleries in London
and Paris speeded up the takeover of the state machinery by the
Bolsheviks, just as the hard-line stance on German reparations
by France in the 1920s made possible the rise of the Nazi Party
under its Führer.

In 2011, unaware or unwilling to factor in the consequences
of cheering on and assisting the crowds that filled the streets
of countries in the Middle East and North Africa (almost in
all cases against leaders who many described as agents of
the US), Secretary of State Hillary Clinton risked the ruling
structures within the GCC. It is not coincidental that the GCC
leadership has since that period sought to broaden their basket
of protectors beyond the members of NATO, in the process
reaching out even to the Sino-Russian alliance. Not that this is

---

[2] M.D. Nalapat, 'Arab Spring to Wahabbi Winter', *Gateway House*, 12 September
2011, https://www.gatewayhouse.in/arab-spring-wahabbi-winter/.

a surprise, for at least in the Middle East, Moscow has stood by friends such as the Assad regime in Damascus in a manner that ensured any effort at regime change by NATO was rendered futile. This has been in contrast to Washington, which has often abandoned long-time friends, including the Kurds in Syria and the Afghan people, to their foes.

The present writer had warned in 2011 itself that the planned collapse of regimes such as those of Syria and Libya would result in an uncontrollable flow of migrants into Europe, and this is what happened. The consequence has been a mass migration into several European countries, not least into Germany, which under Chancellor Angela Merkel permitted in 2015 what could eventually entail three million more people becoming citizens of Germany. The new entrants come from countries in North Africa, the Middle East and parts of South Asia. The ability to turn on or off the tap of uncontrolled migration into Europe has handed President Recep Tayyip Erdogan of Turkey a weapon that is a deterrent to any EU action hostile to him. Just as it took place in Libya once Muammar Gaddafi was deposed in 2011, in Syria the arming, training and funding of 'freedom fighters', many of whom are indistinguishable by their views and actions from the Al-Qaeda or the Taliban, has created a similar flood of refugees out of the country, even while the regime of President Assad has held on with substantial help from Iran and Russia. Whether it be out of overconfidence or naiveté, it would appear from the consequences of some of its actions that the EU has been doing an energetic job of weakening itself, and as a result its geopolitical rivals are intent on exploiting it by actions overt and covert.

Russia was not allowed to be a part of Europe when Boris Yeltsin kept on knocking at the EU's door. The exclusion may have been partly in the view that the chaos of the Yeltsin period would before long lead to a further disintegration of the Russian Federation. However, it was not to be. At the close of 1999, Yeltsin handed over power to Putin, who was from the KGB stable and hence 'unacceptable' to key members of the Atlantic Alliance. Moves to placate Russia were put on hold, and NATO continued to be expanded in a manner that suggested that the Russian Federation was as much of a threat to the alliance as the USSR had been. The entry of Putin into the Kremlin resulted in the Atlantic Alliance once again taking off the table any realistic effort at bridging the strategic distance between itself and the Russian Federation. This may have been a self-goal, for indications are that in the beginning of his stint in power at least, President Putin was respectful of the 'Common European Home' theorem of Gorbachev and the St Petersburg school. He could not but have had knowledge of the many ways in which the security of the USSR had been compromised by the PRC, or the way Beijing, through its activities if not its language, joined Washington to hollow out Russian technological expertise by enticing Russian scientists, engineers and technologists to work in or for China. However, it was a stone wall that Russia faced from the Atlantic Alliance. President Putin accepted from his fourth year in power that the St Petersburg school had been wrong about the European Union collaborating rather than confronting Moscow. The reflex actions he took in Georgia and Ukraine led to sanctions that have turned the Sino-Russian alliance into a reality, at least during the first half of the twenty-first century. The re-emergence of Russia as a potential threat because of Cold War 2.0 between China and the US accompanied by the formation of Russia's 'comprehensive strategic alliance' with China has resulted in other states giving Poland much more influence within NATO, given that it is Poland and the Baltic states and not Germany that share a frontier with the

Russian Federation. Efforts at widening fault lines between Russia and China have yet to take place. Instead, a basket of policies is being implemented by the Atlantic Alliance that is designed to bring them closer.

Determined as the Clinton administration was to further downsize the potential of the geographic giant that had shrunk from the USSR into the Russian Federation, the EU as well as NATO were expanded in a manner which suggested that the threat to the Atlantic Alliance from Moscow was as high as it was from the USSR during the post-war period characterized by Cold War 1.0. The strategic interests of Russia were almost entirely ignored in this expansion. In its rush to incorporate the former Warsaw Pact countries into the EU and NATO without first putting in place durable benchmarks, the chance to ensure a significant change in internal political and societal dynamics from the past was given the go by. The consequence has been that Poland and Hungary, in particular, have relapsed into a form of authoritarianism that is milder than the communist version but considerably at variance with that found in France and other countries that are members of the Atlantic Alliance on the European side. It has been argued that the US lapsed into a form of authoritarianism under President Trump, but this perception was more hype than reality. Now that the Democratic Party has replaced the Republicans in the White House, the cry from the losing side is that 'Big Government' (assumed to be toxic) is back. Certainly, 'Big Spending' was never restrained by successive Republican occupants of the White House, whose record in fiscal rectitude is often less impressive than those of some of their Democratic Party predecessors. A more cautious path towards full membership of former East Bloc countries (except the Baltic states, which needed to be given preference as a special case) in the EU and NATO may have ensured that subsequent developments may have followed a different trajectory at least in the matter of tensions with Russia.

Belarus, Ukraine and Georgia are building blocks in the overall security of the Russian Federation that have long been regarded as essential to protect it from control by potentially hostile countries. The actions of the Kremlin under Putin in these countries is not a surprise when seen in such a light, and while sanctions have had a substantial impact on the Russian economy, they have not moved Moscow away from the strategic gains that it has made in these three countries, sometimes by outright annexation and in other cases by ensuring the rule of proxies in territories (such as in the eastern part of Ukraine) that are regarded as core to the security of the Russian Federation. The possibility of Ukraine moving entirely into the US-led camp in the manner of Poland helped motivate President Putin to annex the Crimea in 2014, something that is not going to be put on the table by Moscow in any future negotiation with Washington. Should Kiev be seen as close to entering the EU and NATO, that is likely to impel most of eastern Ukraine to declare their independence from Ukraine, with an assist from the Russian military that would in turn be assisted off the field by the PRC. As for Belarus, it is going to prove even more fraught with tension and potential conflict, were that country to follow the example of post-Yanukovych Ukraine and reverse its policy of closeness to the Russian Federation. The Indo-Pacific is now a more important theatre than the Atlantic, and it is China and not Russia that is the primary threat to the US-led alliance. This being so, the expansion of the range and membership of the EU and NATO that was witnessed during the Clinton and George W. Bush tenures in the White House needs to finally end. Should the contrary occur, it would be another self-goal by the EU (and its transoceanic partner) that would strengthen the already tightening grip of Beijing over the strategic space of Moscow and give the Kremlin even less to lose from NATO's perception of 'bad behaviour' than is already the case.

6

After Twentieth-Century Travail, Eurasia Enters the Twenty-First

Wars are caused by a combination of objective and subjective circumstances. It is impossible to refute that the 1919 Treaty of Versailles, drawn towards the end of World War I, contained conditions certain to inflame passions in Germany. The hardship faced by the Germans after the war was attributed by them to the treaty, and therefore to the nations aligned against Germany, notably France and Britain. The Weimar Republic erred in seeking to meet the impossible obligations imposed by the Allied powers, giving way to the Nazi state in 1933. Rather than confront an initially weak Germany once the country came under the control of Adolf Hitler, an individual who had made little secret of his hunger for war, the Allied powers adopted a conciliatory and forgiving stance, which had been denied to the moderate politicians of the Weimar Republic. The 'historical injustice' done to Germany by the Treaty of Versailles (together with its perceived need for *Lebensraum*) got cited by Chancellor Hitler as a justification for the wars he inevitably launched. By 1936, when Britain together with France and their armed forces sat on their hands when 20,000 German troops re-occupied the Rhineland, it was clear that the Treaty of Versailles was a dead letter even to Paris and London. Churchill may not have been right in his conclusions about India but was entirely correct about the need for the US, France and Britain to take on Nazi Germany before that country became uncontrollable in the manner that Churchill forecast would occur under the 'Nazis'. After 1936 came the 1938 German annexation of the Sudeten territories that historically belonged to Czechoslovakia. This time, such aggression was not merely ignored but actively facilitated by France and Britain.

The news after the Sudetenland occupation began to transform public opinion in Britain in the direction of the Churchillians, although not in France. Even in the former, the almost subterranean change in public mood from appeasement to confrontation was not enough to make British sounds better Prime Minister Neville Chamberlain bring Churchill back into his Council of Ministers. That awaited the declaration of war on Germany by Britain and France in 1939 following the invasion by Germany of Poland. Interestingly, the Polish government had insistently warned Paris and London not to come to an agreement with Moscow to jointly take action against Berlin, convinced that Stalin was a greater danger than Hitler was to the Poles. The opposition of Warsaw to any pact with Moscow was a factor that greatly assisted the subsequent takeover of Poland by Hitler, joined immediately afterwards by Stalin. In the present day, the tenacity with which Warsaw is pursuing a hard line against the Kremlin is making negotiated peace seem difficult between Russia and Ukraine. The risk of the intensification of the war until Putin's surrender that Poland seeks, morphing into Russian attacks on Polish territory is real. Should this take place, the options before the US, in particular, will range from awful to horrible.

Leaving aside the pseudo-science of 'Race Theory', there was no objective reason for the German Führer to order the Holocaust which took away the lives of six million Jews, not to mention countless Roma and others judged by the Nazis to be undeserving of existence, including the physically and mentally challenged within the 'Aryan' community. The Jewish community in Germany was substantially assimilated within the general population, at least in comparison to other euro-ethnic countries, save perhaps the US and Britain. They possessed a variety of intellectual gifts that would have proved invaluable in wartime, just as they were during World War I to Germany and were to the US after a few managed to escape to that country from Nazi-occupied Europe.

After the takeover of Czechoslovakia, Germany could have negotiated with Poland for access to East Prussia, perhaps through an exchange of territory. This would have affirmed the view that Graham Allison's warning of the Thucydides Trap[1] is not inevitable, and that a rising power could come to an understanding with its competitor without resorting to kinetic force. The problem comes when the head of government of the rising power has a subjective propensity towards aggressive action rather than negotiation. This is based on the belief that much more would be gained through the use of coercion backed by kinetic force than by negotiation without the use of such methods.

Judging by the trajectory followed by CPC General Secretary Xi since he took over the leadership of the CPC

---

[1] Thucydides Trap, or Thucydides' Trap, is a term popularized by American political scientist Graham T. Allison to describe an apparent tendency towards war when an emerging power threatens to displace an existing great power as a regional or international hegemon. It was coined and is primarily used to describe a potential conflict between the United States and the People's Republic of China.

of China, the PLA has superseded the Ministry of Foreign Affairs in several matters of external policy, and the Central Committee of the CPC is proving no match in influencing the mind of Xi as much as the CMC does. Comparisons with the past are inexact, even characterizations of the very different dynamic of US-PRC rivalry during Cold War 2.0 from the USSR-US dynamic that was played out during Cold War 1.0. The reason for the use of the Cold War label nevertheless is the ease with which essential features of the new situation would be understood by the wider public as a consequence of their familiarity with the term 'Cold War'. Clearly, the PRC is not the USSR, nor is the CPC similar in chemistry or in its functioning and tactics to the manner that the CPSU was during the period it was in power in the Soviet Union. Nor is Xi Jinping a modern version of Stalin, nor is his ideology and thinking similar to that of the Soviet Vozhd (leader), though there is somewhat more congruence between the basics of Xi Jinping thought and Mao Zedong thought. In contrast to Deng, who was able to ensure not a Long March but a Long Peace for China, given his mindset, Mao was constantly involved in various situations of conflict both within the country and with outside powers, including with the US. Such is the case with Xi.

Whether the Thucydides Trap is activated or not hinges majorly on the personality of the leader of the rising power, especially if she or he has powers that are close to dictatorial. Such a level was never reached even by President Trump, a natural autocrat who was blocked by the governance system of his country on hugely consequential steps attempted by him, such as seeking a Moscow-Washington alliance to confront Beijing, or in reversing the decision of the electors in the 2020 US presidential polls. This stands in contrast to the situation in

China. In an uncompromising approach, Xi sees it as his duty to 'reclaim' land and water space that was never in the possession of China. Three locations where a rising probability exists of kinetic conflict (in one of which such clashes have already been initiated) are Taiwan, the South China Sea and the Himalayan massif. In Taiwan's case, previous general secretaries of the CPC as well as Chairman Mao himself declined to set a firm timetable for absorption within the PRC of the Republic of China, which more and more is being referred to more accurately, as Taiwan in international discourse. Rather than an expansion in the proportion of Taiwanese citizens who favour unification with the PRC, Xi's aggressive behaviour has led to that number shrinking.

Among the reasons for this is the effective scrapping by Xi in 2020 of the Hong Kong 'One Country Two Systems' model. Wary of the risk of the spread of public support for any model different from that followed in the PRC and having within its fold a territory (Hong Kong) separate from it in much administrative and judicial practice, General Secretary Xi made the Hong Kong Special Administrative Region indistinguishable from the Macau Special Administrative Region, which has long been autonomous only in name. Given his preference for uniformity across the country, it is clear what Xi Jinping has in mind for Taiwan—it is not One Country Three Systems (which was touted by some analysts fifteen years ago as a formula for the peaceful absorption of Taiwan) or even One Country Two Systems, but One Country, One System. This may have helped several inhabitants of Taiwan in making up their minds about the need to preserve the independence of their island nation. Jiang Zemin, CPC general secretary (1989–2002), and Hu Jintao, CPC general secretary (2002–12) offered concessions and facilities to induce not Taiwanese businesses merely, but also its people to settle in China, even while numerous brides from the PRC joined the families of their Taiwanese husbands. The problem facing Xi is that most of these brides have begun to prefer the freedoms they enjoy in their new country over the restrictions that are becoming more rather than less onerous in the country of their birth. A smaller proportion of children born of PRC-Taiwan couples, especially those living in the island nation, prefer unification to the de facto independence that Taiwan has retained despite pressure from Beijing.

Just as was the case under Mao, life under Xi is becoming more fraught with risk and uncertainty. Some in the CPC get on a fast track in their careers while others land in jail, and there seems no discernible pattern why a Zhou goes to jail while his friend Wang gets a promotion. Taiwan has its judicial risks, such as hyperactive prosecutors looking for the publicity attendant on incarcerating big names in business or politics. However, the level of palpable judicious and administrative arbitrariness in the democracy across the strait is much less than is the case with the PRC, particularly now that the bigger country is under a leader who consciously seeks to emulate the Great Helmsman who founded the PRC in 1949 and led it until his death in 1975. During the period when Mao Zedong led the PRC, the dominant motif was Han nationalism and PRC exceptionalism. It was an end to the 'Century of Humiliation' and the eventual ascent of China to the centre of world geopolitics, the Middle Kingdom brought back to its previous glory.

The subtext of such a message was that rule by the CPC led by Mao was essential to the eventual success of such an outcome. After the Mao era ended, Deng Xiaoping changed the emphasis from glory on the outside to a better life internally. The compact between the people and the Party was that their lives would improve, and in turn, they would accept the hold of the CPC over their lives and the country, which during Mao's time had from the 1940s almost doubled in territory from what it had been in earlier times.

The World Health Organization (WHO) appears to have been very forgiving about China's role in disseminating SARS Cov-2 across the world after local authorities failed between December 2019 and January 2020 to confine the Covid-19 outbreak within Hubei province. Interestingly, among those who ensured substantial funding for the Wuhan Institute of Virology (WIV) in its research into how that virus could be made even more deadly was Dr Anthony Fauci, who has followed the trajectory of Federal Bureau of Investigation (FBI) Lifetime Director J. Edgar Hoover in remaining a fixture within successive US administrations, including those of Trump and Biden. An associate who joined him in ensuring such funding was Dr Peter Daszak, who nevertheless was among those tasked by the WHO to proceed to Wuhan more than a year after the pandemic had started to find out its origins. Unsurprisingly, Dr Daszak gave a clean bill of health to the Wuhan Institute, lapsing almost into poetry at the state-of-the-art standards of the institute, somehow managing to forget that what was relevant was not the standards of January 2021 but the circumstances a year and earlier, when even he had raised red flags about the manner in which some procedures were being carried out. In the WIV, fantastical theories involving multiple countries were certified as probable by the WHO team after their visit to the PRC and getting access to only such data as were shown to them by the authorities there, a situation somehow accepted by the team as sufficient transparency. Much of the world has moved away from the WHO view on the non-culpability of agencies in the PRC. Just as the 2008 financial crash had a severe effect on confidence in the financial system and the profit-seeking methods of key bankers in the Atlantic Alliance, the Covid-19 pandemic had a substantial downward effect on perceptions about the PRC across the world. Instead of policy changes designed to win back such lost goodwill, the PRC has been doubling down on the very behaviour that has caused such an increase in unease about the rise of China in major world capitals. Interestingly, in a way similar to Mao Zedong thought, the message implicit in Xi Jinping thought is that only he has the vision and grit to restore Middle Kingdom status to China.

The Mao Zedong primer followed by Xi mandates international respect as part of factors that would go towards ensuring the acquiescence of citizens of the PRC towards the CPC leadership. Judging by the way a military-oriented strategy has been promoted by General Secretary Xi, it has become necessary for the public to accept it to ensure that their country is not simply respected but feared. This is the consequence of the military muscle that has increasingly been put on display in the PRC since 2012. In contrast, Jiang Zemin as CPC general secretary largely observed Deng's dictum of 'speaking softly and hiding the big stick'. In contrast to Deng's non-kinetic methods, from the time that Hu Jintao entered his second five-year term as CPC general secretary in 2008 (coinciding with the Wall Street-created financial meltdown of substantial private wealth across the world), an 'expansion by stealth' took place amid the welter of failing confidence in western financial markets, especially in the South China Sea but also on a smaller scale elsewhere, including in the Himalayan massif. Almost all of this took place in a piecemeal manner that made it possible even for the countries directly affected to essentially look the other way, including India and the members of ASEAN.

Soon after Xi Jinping took over in 2012, the creeping pace got converted into a trot in all three flashpoints, thereby making it more difficult for the governments of the countries involved to respond merely in a formal or perfunctory manner that in substance ignored the transgressions and the creeping loss of land and sea territories. Such an acceleration in the expansionist policy became prominent by 2017, when India and China came close to a shooting war over Bhutanese territory (the Doklam stand-off) that Beijing claimed was part of the PRC. Intrusions into Taiwanese airspace multiplied, as well as intensification of the PRC-sponsored exclusion of Taiwan from international fora (no matter by what name it agreed to be called, such as 'Chinese Taipei'). The construction of military facilities was speeded up on bits of land either artificially created in the South China Sea at substantial expense or simply occupied by the PLA, as along the Himalayan massif. In 2020, despite the effects of SARS Cov-2 on the global economy, such assertive behaviour intensified, with even Chinese diplomats adopting a militaristic tone in their public utterances.

The world is witnessing what happens when the leadership of a rising power increasingly turns to military force to assure its ascent to the top, and supplements or precedes that by info war and the covert use of cyberspace to make domestic differences of opinion in target countries (including the US and India) more toxic. The first four decades of twentieth-century Europe furnish an answer to such a query. What is being witnessed in Asia is a rising power that seeks to not just consolidate but expand on its successes by whatever means it considers will achieve its purposes. Miscalculation of the extent to which countries affected would look away from such transgressions has been the cause of many wars, including the two World Wars.

The second great war of the previous century triggered by Germany began in Europe with its annexation of Czechoslovakia in 1938 and in Asia by Japan's invasion of China soon after its 1931 occupation of the then distinct entity of Manchuria. A principal reason behind the huge escalation of these conflicts was that the major powers directly not involved in what was seen by them as localized conflicts failed to understand that such flashpoints could, if allowed to continue, mark the start of a conflict that would involve them at a later date. There was passive acceptance by the (then much more powerful) French military together with the (equally supine) British of the Wehrmacht's occupation of the Rhineland in 1936. Pushing Hitler's army back by force would have imploded his appeal in Germany and spared the world much future grief. In 1938, Prime Ministers Neville Chamberlain (UK) and Daladier (France) not only declined to oppose the seizure of Czech territory by the Nazi leader but laid out a welcome mat for him during the process. It was logical for Hitler to believe that no matter how active he was in Germany's east, there would not be a military response from France or Britain. Neither Paris nor London understood the consequences of the subjective hostility of the post-1933 German leadership to not just Soviet ideology but their own, albeit applicable only to what they defined as 'civilized' people and not to the population of the colonies they controlled. In much the same fashion, all but a few policymakers in Delhi, Washington, Tokyo, London and other such capitals have failed to have grasped the implications of the foundations of the 'Weltanschauung' of the CPC, and the efforts of General Secretary Xi since his takeover of the party to get it actualized within his period in office. They have persisted in the approach of giving greater, much greater, importance in terms of predictive analysis of the periphery of CPC ideology and leadership objectives than to the core, even though the latter characteristic has been substantially brought into the open by Xi.

The global consequences to the US in the event of its being surpassed by the PRC as a technological, economic and military power are obvious, hence the fading charm in Washington of a return to the 'business and concessions' period exemplified during the presidency of Bill Clinton. At the same time, the changes in the chemistry of the population of the PRC since the Deng reforms went into operation in the 1980s and the shift in attitudes to increased hardship from stoic acceptance to dismay have made it mandatory for the CPC leadership to continue to deliver economic progress. This needs to be done in a world made more complex by the coming into clearer focus of the competing interests of Beijing and Washington. Because of his failure in this, Xi has reverted to the Lin Biao playbook of 'enemies seeking to choke China' and therefore the need for 'struggle and austerity' to overcome such plots.

While Mao did make efforts to spread the gospel of revolutionary change to other countries, including in India through support in the 1960s to the 'Naxalbari' movement, Deng adopted his own version of Stalin's 'socialism in one country'. The Soviet dictator rubbished the theories of Leon Trotsky about the need to spread revolutionary ideology across the world and was in favour of consolidating at home the power of the CPSU led by him, ironically as Stalin was. Deng Xiaoping concentrated his efforts to build up the PRC as an economic force in which the dominant position of the CPC would be as secure as the economic future of the inhabitants of the country he led. The process begun under General Secretary Hu Jintao and visibly and aggressively promoted by his successor in the job has been to try and bring more and more countries around to the view that the adoption of key elements of the PRC model of governance would promote economic welfare far better than reliance on the 'liberal' market model touted by the Washington Consensus. The 2008 financial crash caused by the limitless greed of Wall Street operators opened the way for the Beijing Consensus to challenge the Washington Consensus.

What was not recognized at the time but has become clearer now, is that the Washington versus Beijing 'clash of consensus building' was the first obvious sign that there was indeed a clash of systems between the US and the PRC that has begun to be acknowledged as Cold War 2.0. This will prove as existential a contest as Cold War 1.0 was, although the eventual winner is yet not certain. Policymakers who brush aside the reality and the possible consequences of Cold War 2.0 are in effect saying that Czechoslovakia in 1938 ought not to have been prevented but repeated in Poland in 1939 and thereafter. In brief, the contention of Cold War 2.0 deniers is that the US and its allies should concede the inevitability of PRC primacy and accept the consequences to themselves and other countries of such a decision. Once General Secretary Xi substituted the indeterminate timelines for the expansion of the spaces beyond those that are within the internationally accepted boundaries of the PRC, he revealed his intent of accelerating these alterations and changing the timeline for PRC global primacy so that this occurs during his stint in office. Which is why his systemic battle with the countries that would be adversely affected by such a transformation became an inevitable response from the democracies that would slow down, reverse and finally eliminate such expansionism and usurpation of sovereignty of countries that are Xi's Cold War 2.0 targets.

During the 1939–45 conflict, the German side was affected by its prioritization of (a) the psychotic elimination by Nazi Germany of the Jewish population; (b) ensuring a 'peacetime' lifestyle for the civilian population as far as was possible during the war; and (c) the brutal treatment and exploitation of occupied countries, a policy that drained away any sparks of genuine compliance in occupied countries with the interests of Nazi Germany. Constraints have been placed on PRC economic performance by the rising barriers to economic expansion owing to geopolitical shifts partly caused by Xi's complete implementation of what he regards as the CPC's core objectives. As a consequence, in place of the far more generous approach adopted by Mao to poorer countries especially in Africa, that followed by his successors has been 'extractive'. In other words, they are policies designed to extract as much from a country as would contribute to economic expansion in the home country. This has been the case with the US and India as well, from where massive trade surpluses have been generated, as also to a lesser extent with the EU, whereas in the case of the Middle East or Australia, 'extraction' describes a process by which such territories contribute to the economic success of the PRC through sale of natural resources.

Although cloaked in sugary phrases, the reality of 'extractive' geopolitics (with its attendant geo-economics) has created networks of influencers in several countries that are uneasy with the consequences to themselves and to the people at large through increasing engagement with China. This is leading several to drift towards still nascent bloc of countries that are moving towards acting in concert with the US to blunt the ascent of the world's East Asian superpower. While Pakistan is known (except by a few sentimentalists in think tanks of London, New York and Washington) to be safely in the PRC orbit, the reality is that the CMC-inspired policy by Beijing of relying on the Pakistan military as its pillar of support has distanced Beijing from the growing number of citizens of that country who look upon the military as a parasitical block towards economic well-being and sociopolitical reform. The army in Pakistan is firmly under the domination of those from the Pothohar region of Punjab, and as a consequence, has lost substantial goodwill among the Baloch, Sindhis and even Pashtuns. This has led to a similar loss of goodwill among such groups towards the primary force multiplier for the Pakistan military, which is China. The exceptionally close relationship between GHQ Rawalpindi and the PLA is mirrored by the relationship between the two governments.

Pakistan became a nuclear proxy of the PRC, designed (almost certainly with the tacit consent if not connivance of the US) at first to help coax India into giving up its domestically built nuclear capability if Pakistan did the same. After this gambit failed during the Clinton presidency, the focus shifted to the generation of an ambience of nuclear menace and blackmail such as would deter India from a sufficiently strong conventional response to the numerous wounds sought to be inflicted by GHQ Rawalpindi. Aware that the only other 'tiger on the mountain' with the potential to challenge its primacy in Asia is India, the manner in which the Pakistan military could—and did—keep its rival distracted and busy in firefighting, diverted its attention away from the source of the threat, which was the CMC-inspired overall PRC line on India. Now that Pakistan is proving less effective in such an endeavour, more attention is being given as to how Moscow can serve to blunt any action by India designed to counter the plans of the CMC of the

CPC towards it, especially through forging a close security alliance with the US.

Among the factors working in favour of Beijing is the manner in which the concept of 'balance' (that in effect means an effort at reconciling opposites) is central to strategic thought in the Lutyens Zone. The central ethos of this is not the break from the mindset of the past as ought to have been the case, but a continuation of the colonial-era view that the general public in India is incapable of handling major responsibility by themselves, and hence need constant and intrusive state supervision. The chokehold of the administrative services and the complex of British-era laws and regulations that have been added on to rather than subtracted in the intervening years since 1947 have held back the country from actualizing much of its potential. Most of what has been achieved has been despite, rather than because of, an administrative structure that the political class in India has been in awe of since the era of Nehru and Patel. Although there were murmurs of comprehensive administrative reforms to be attempted by Prime Minister Modi from 2014, thus far these have been less substantial than needed, although incremental change has been made, most notably in efforts at using digital technologies to improve the quality of governance.

Just as the PRC needs to deal with the obstacle of the US to achieve the goal of global primacy, India is PRC's obstacle to the secure unobstructed primacy in Asia. Ensuring that Washington and Delhi remain apart and do not work in sync with each other to thwart the PRC is a central focus of PRC diplomacy, sought to be actualized not just directly but also through partners, of which the most prominent in such a role is Russia. The gravitational pull of a comprehensive US-India partnering in the constrainment of the PRC would have a significant impact on several other countries in Asia. Not least because in kinetic terms, the US and India, assisted by countries such as Japan, Indonesia and Vietnam, would prevail against the Sino-Russian alliance in establishing a balance of power in the Indo-Pacific that prevents the hegemony of the PRC.

7

The Setting: Twenty-First-Century Asia's Uneasy Equilibrium

Discussion on the 'Asian Century' has been widespread, and it is a reality that the continent has surpassed Europe and North America in several metrics of comprehensive global power. Signs of this were visible from the start of the twentieth century, beginning with the destruction of the Russian fleet by the Japanese navy in 1905 at Tsushima, and continuing in Japan's military overcoming of European powers in Southeast Asia in the 1940s. Later came the successful conclusion of the Indonesian, Israeli and Indian freedom struggles. The holding to a draw by China and North Korea of the US and South Korea in the Korean War and the victory of the Vietnamese under Ho Chi Minh first against France and later against the US indicated that Asia was on the road towards reclaiming its traditional status as the lead continent. It became clear that the centre point of global attention would shift from the shores of the Atlantic to those of the Indo-Pacific in the final decade of the twentieth century. Of course, it took a decade more before that reality became widely accepted, and another decade more before the Atlantic Alliance powers on the European side of that ocean began to acknowledge such a tectonic shift. Every continent is less a reflection of inter-country similarities than it is a catch-all geographic concept, and such a reality holds particular salience in the case of Asia, by far the largest and most populous continent on the globe. Once again, the continent has become the most developed in terms of overall national productivity, a disproportion expected to intensify during the coming decades.

At Asia's western edge is Turkey, long a wannabe European country that seems finally to have reconciled itself to its exclusion from the 'Common European Home'. Such a divergence is not because of ethnicity, for significant elements of the population in the south of Europe are indistinguishable from the Turkish population. Nor is it the consequence of historical memories dating from the Ottoman period and its invasions into some European states of the Turkish military, recollections that are particularly vivid in the case of countries such as Armenia and to a lesser extent, Austria. The publicly unspoken reason why Turkey has thus far been kept out of the European Union is not just the size and rate of growth of the Turkish population but the faith to which they belong, Islam. In a less obvious way, any increase in the religious consciousness of the Turkish people vis-à-vis Islam (and President Erdogan has been energetic in fanning such a sentiment, more on account of his politics than his faith) is followed by similar piety found in much of Europe where the different strands of the Christian faith are concerned, especially in regions to the south and east of that continent. Whether entry into the EU would have dampened the advance towards religious exclusivism that is taking place in Erdogan-led Turkey at the expense of secular values remains indeterminate. What is clear is that the Erdogan years have widened the societal difference between Turkey and the EU so significantly that talk of Ankara joining the EU has almost completely disappeared from both sides.

Marx had written in his 'The 18th Brumaire of Louis Bonaparte' that history repeats itself first as tragedy and later as farce. This is what has been happening to Turkey as a consequence of the strategic ambitions of Erdogan. The head of the present government in Turkey has sought to revive the glories of the Ottoman era, bypassing the period of reform introduced with the advent of Mustafa Kemal Ataturk in 1923.[1] In the latter half of the twentieth century, Turkish field marshal Mustafa Kemal Ataturk's reforms were weakened not just by religious fundamentalists but partly by the (then) secular military. Throughout the 1950s, Menderes, as the head of the Turkish government, sought to make permanent the Ataturk reforms, but the military became wary of his popularity and deposed him in 1960, in the process installing a regime that snuffed out basic rights and set the country on a course to stagnation.

The hold of the Turkish military over the political process came to an end in 2002 with the victory of the AKP (*Adalet ve Kalkınma Partisi* or Justice and Development Party) under Erdogan, who used the cover of EU backing to ensure the emasculation of secular generals. In hindsight, it is apparent that this was not out of any concern for democratic values but based on the new leader's desire to anchor his country in religious traditions prevalent in the Arab world. Supported by the UK and subsequently by the US, Arab forces swearing fealty to the newly enunciated tenets of Wahhabism overcame Ottoman overlordship during and after the 1914–19 world war. The next significant victory of Wahhabism, this time over the very ethos of Turkey, is the manner in which the tenets of Abdel

---

[1] Michael Colborne and Maxim Edwards, 'Erdogan Is Making the Ottoman Empire Great Again', *Foreign Policy*, June 22, 2018, https://foreignpolicy.com/2018/06/22/erdogan-is-making-the-ottoman-empire-great-again/.

Wahhab have been adapted and promoted by the Erdogan administration, which has sought to mainstream them across Turkey, in the process seeking to replace the Sufi orientation of his people.

Islam is demographically on course to overtake Christianity as the faith having the greatest number of adherents in the world well before the middle of the twenty-first century.[2] Given such numbers, the resonance of appeals based on the 'Islam in danger' theme is difficult to comprehend. Judging by social media posts, there appear to be some Muslim citizens of India who regard not simply themselves but their faith as being under threat in India, a sentiment that was earlier used to devastating effect in the 1930s, and which led to the partition of India based on faith in 1947. Across the world, the proportion of Muslims who are entering the ranks of the top tier of doctors, scientists and cultural greats is growing, as is the proportion of women who in increasing numbers are not just being educated as fully as their male relatives but are as successful as the latter in their careers. A reason for optimism is the fight-back against Wahhabi tenets initiated by Saudi Arabian Crown Prince Mohammed bin Salman and the manner in which women in Iran are throwing off not only their veils but fear of the clerical overlordship that has been throttling progress in that land of ancient traditions.

In the knowledge economy of the twenty-first century, the public needs to accept that living and working in a multicultural and multi-faith environment is necessary for the stability and regeneration of a country. Although much has been said about the 'explosive' rates of growth of the Muslim population in

---

[2] 'The Future of World Religions: Population Growth Projections, 2010–2050', Pew Research Center, April 2, 2015, https://www.pewforum.org/2015/04/02/religious-projections-2010-2050/.

India, the reality is that income, awareness and education are having the same effect on average family size in Muslim families as they have on Hindu, Christian, Buddhist or other families. The total number of Muslims (who, just as in the case of their counterparts in other faiths, are overwhelmingly moderate and welcoming of modernity) has begun to stabilize as a consequence of rising education and income levels within the community. Unlike in the case of Pakistan, where Wahhabism has been imposed on the governance and educational system by the military since the 1970s, Wahhabism has not been able to gain traction in India, although it has made considerable progress in Bangladesh because of the lingering theological influence that was propagated by the Pakistan military and spread among the local Muslims.

Given that Asia is home to a substantial share of the Muslim population of the globe—Indonesia, Pakistan and India having the three largest Muslim populations anywhere—the ongoing battle for adherents between moderate, mainstream Islam and Wahhabism is of prime significance to societal stability and economic growth. An encouraging sign is that youth overall are flocking to modern education wherever they can find it. Including in Iran and Saudi Arabia, the two countries which are the home of Wahhabism-Khomeinism (W-K), the young have moved away from clerics who fill their minds and lives with ritual and reject the imperative of reform. Contact with global trends and ideas via the worldwide web has ensured that the narrow focus that is sought to be mandated in institutions promoting the superficially diverse but essentially similar ideologies of Wahhabism and Khomeinism face competition from concepts, many introduced through the internet. This has been factored in by those eager to extend the hold of fundamentalism, and their response has been to seek to fill cyberspace with their logic and teachings. A contrary effort by the modern, moderate majority of Muslims to counter and overwhelm this invasion of cyberspace discourse by the Wahhabi-Khomeinist fringe is still far from the levels needed. It is a matter of astonishment and satisfaction that within the Al Saud family that rules Saudi Arabia, a fightback against Wahhabism has finally been launched, led by the crown prince. This has long been overdue, for fossil fuels are increasingly likely to be replaced by 'clean' technologies. Once the batteries for items such as electric vehicles pass the price barrier into a zone of low cost and greater convenience, the discarding of fossil fuels will accelerate to a point where their use becomes minuscule.

Turkey has endured two decades and counting under Erdogan, who has acted the way he has as a consequence of two postulates. The first relates to an increase in his popularity among Muslims worldwide—it will ensure a flood of investment from Arab and other Muslim high net worth individuals (HNIs) into Turkey, thereby ensuring high growth rates. The other is that the geographical position of his country and its utility to NATO will shield his regime from any other than the mild S-400 sanctions imposed by President Trump in the closing days of 2020. President Trump enabled Turkey to escape with a slap on the wrist after the installation of S-400 systems from the Russian Federation, thereby making it more attractive for first India and afterwards perhaps countries in the Middle East to go in for the S-400 system. This is especially so in view of the steep price tag placed by President Trump and his successor, Biden, on alternative US air surveillance and defence systems, despite how important they are to the security of the Indo-Pacific. A greater focus on security needs rather than the accumulation of cash would have resulted in a much better network of US-built THAAD systems in Asia and Africa than has been the case thus far.

Ayatollah Khomeini believed that the way to the Muslim heart lay in comprehensive support to those who believed that Israel should be eliminated from the map and its Jewish population dispersed to locations outside the region. President Erdogan sees in his embrace of Wahhabism the key to political traction within the Arab world (and in his calculations, accompanying financial investment). Given the importance of Wahhabism needing to be 'capped, rolled back and eliminated' (to paraphrase the Clinton administration on India's nuclear weapons programme), that the rest of NATO has thus far declined to act against Erdogan may be attributed to the fear of consequential action (such as incentivizing another flood of Syrian and other refugees from Turkey into Europe, conveniently via Greece). At a time when key elements of the Al Sauds ruling the Kingdom of Saudi Arabia (KSA) are moving away from their long-standing backing of Wahhabism, or when youth in Iran are turning their backs on retrogressive clerics, that Turkey under Erdogan has abandoned its Kemalist past, and its Sufi heritage, presents a problem not just for Asia but for the rest of the world as well.

Ankara is in competition with Riyadh to win over the hearts and minds of the billion-plus global Muslim population. The vision of modernization now being promoted by reform-minded members of the ruling family of Saudi Arabia is far more attractive to the young across the Middle East than a radicalism that since the last century has caused a surfeit of pain. The ascendance of reformist elements within the ruling dynasty in KSA, added to the fact that Mecca and Medina are both located in the kingdom, makes it difficult to understand President Erdogan's apparent confidence that Ankara can replace Riyadh as the special place that the country has in Muslim hearts and minds. This is a battle of competing visions, in which the advantage remains with Saudi Arabia. Despite their prioritizing of securing the goodwill of the Arab peoples over the (more numerous) Muslim community in South Asia, Malaysia and Indonesia, neither Iran nor Turkey is likely to have the dominant geopolitical or even cultural impact over the Arab world that their leaders seek. Neither country is Arab, and since the birth of Prophet Muhammad, the Arab people together with their language and culture have regarded themselves as a privileged niche within the global Muslim population, an advantage in perception that Iran or Turkey cannot match. Rather than indulge Erdogan in the manner that the Atlantic Alliance has, the sooner he is brought to account for in effect abandoning the founding principles of not just the Kemalist state but NATO, the better for the success of the moderate, modern side in the global contest between moderate and Wahhabi or Khomeinist theologies within the Muslim population.

The KSA, Turkey and Iran have been regarded as the principal players in the Middle East, but there is a fourth, Israel. The modern state that was established in 1948 and the civilization that was re-established in the region of its birth after two millennia has since the 1950s been an important part of regional dynamics. Its upward trajectory in terms of scientific prowess and technological achievement have made Israel an outlier in a region almost totally dependent on foreign technology. Such prowess makes the country important in steering countries in its vicinity away from dependence on petro product exports for their economic salience, a fact recognized in the Abraham Accords that have been signed between Israel and some Arab states since 2020.

There was a Two State solution designed in the 1948 partition of the Palestinian territories, although this has for long not been accepted as 'legitimate' by some countries on the grounds that the separation of Israel from Palestine was based on religion. The countries making this argument are at the same time enthusiastic backers of Pakistan, a country that was created by the same British overlords in 1947 explicitly based on faith. This is symptomatic of the mindset of those in charge of Palestine at the time of the formation of the State of Israel. They with their backers abroad launched a war against the Jewish state in 1948 that ended in an expansion of the territory of Israel. Another war in 1967 produced a similar result, while that launched in 1973 failed to achieve any reduction in the territory controlled by the Jewish state. Egypt and Jordan read the tea leaves correctly and established state-to-state relations with Israel. This was not to the liking of those who believed that such a move should follow the withdrawal of Israel to the borders it had before the 1967 war launched not by Tel Aviv but by Cairo and its allies. Such an impossible condition set for Israel (of moving back to the pre-1967 borders) is similar to those sought to be imposed on India as a precondition for assistance by the UK-US (Harriman-Sandys) mission that followed the 1962 war between China and India.

In the final months of the Trump administration, several other Arab states followed the example of Amman and Cairo and normalized relations with Israel, a development that is among the few foreign policy achievements of the 45th President of the US. Ironically, its very success in the field of battle may have the effect of its leaders adopting a reconciliatory approach towards the Arab minority in Israel, given the importance of the Israeli Arab vote in the absence of a consolidation of the Jewish vote that has never happened in an election. Multi-cornered contests, in which the Arab parties are likely to continue to have a prominent role in a coalition government, are likely to become the norm in a country that protects its tradition of democratic dissent almost as fiercely as it does its security. In time, perhaps such an influence will prod Jerusalem into giving the Palestinian authority enough power to leverage the human potential of the Palestinian people in creating a state that, though small in area, would have a prosperous economy. Such an outcome in the choppy Israel-Palestine cross-currents would be deserving of attention by the 46th President of the US, besides friends of the Jewish state such as India. A friendly relationship between Israel and its neighbours in the region would be to the benefit of both and deprive extremists of what is among the most-used arguments they employ in their constant effort to recruit youths into extremist groups. In such a context, the 2020 Abraham Accords[3] that saw the establishment of normal state-to-state ties between more Arab states and Israel was a mutually beneficial development.

The battle taking place within more than a billion Muslim hearts and minds is that being waged by the moderate and modernizing majority of the Muslim faith against those who remain committed to W-K. As yet, Khomeinism is unlike Wahhabism in not being a significant threat to almost all countries. A significant exception is the State of Israel, to whom Khomeinism is the biggest threat. This is what explains the obsession of the leaders of Israel about Iran under the clerical order.

A way in which W-K is steadily getting hyphenated in practice is the rising possibility of Turkey and Iran coming closer. The two major powers have in recent years been moving

---

[3] The Abraham Accords was signed by Israel, the United Arab Emirates and Bahrain on September 15, 2020. The agreement aims to regularize diplomatic, economic and cultural bonds among these nations with a significant impact on Middle Eastern geopolitics. The Government of the United States acted as mediator throughout negotiations for this historic accord.

closer to the Sino-Russian alliance even as they continue
to move apart from the rival group of countries centred on
Washington. Both have a mutual antipathy to Saudi Arabia
and, in particular, to Crown Prince Mohammed bin Salman.
Turkey under Erdogan has moved away from anything other
than a pro forma adherence to NATO. At the same time, the
sanctions imposed on Iran and in large part retained since
the 1979–81 hostage crisis involving the takeover of the US
embassy in Tehran by Khomeini's supporters have succeeded
in keeping the Persian-speaking country distant from the
Atlantic Alliance, with the exception of a brief thaw consequent
on the signing of the JCPOA in 2015. This was repudiated by
President Trump in 2018. Given the lack of empathy of much
of the population of Iran with the clerical masters of Iran
and the importance of that country in the region of which
it is a prominent part, the absence of any workable, long-
term strategy on the part of Washington to win over Tehran
is puzzling except in the context of clerical Iran's aggressive
stance on Israel.

Any normalization of ties with the US would require the
abandonment by the clerics of Iran of their oft-expressed policy
of seeking the downfall of the only Jewish-majority country in
the world. Such a fixation makes even less sense in the twenty-
first century than it may have in an earlier period, given Israel's
own defensive and offensive military capabilities, which have
made impossible any serious pursuit through conventional and
non-conventional means by Iran and any presumed ally of the
clerical order of the attempted destruction of the Jewish state.
Israel is here to stay, and more and more countries in its vicinity
are understanding this and adapting policies to take account of
this reality. Rather than the State of Israel, it is Iran that has
suffered enormously from the Khomeinist policy of obsessive

hostility towards Israel and the range of actions against that country that have flowed consequent to such a tenet.

It is not within the broader Middle East and North Africa that the majority of the world's Muslims reside, but in the Indian subcontinent and Indonesia—Malaysia can be added to this group. The battle for supremacy between the Wahhabi and Khomeinist theologies and the moderate version of a great faith is being fought not just in the broader Middle East but in the Indian subcontinent, Malaysia and Indonesia. Fortunately, with the exception of parts of Pakistan and to a lesser extent segments in Bangladesh, it is moderation and modernism that seems to be prevailing in youth, over the effort of religious supremacists to popularize exclusivist doctrines based on the concept of religious supremacy. India, Indonesia, Bangladesh and Malaysia need to work closer together to establish a denser network of economic, cultural and people-to-people exchanges, especially between Indonesia and India. A common factor is the battle against colonial oppression. Unlike Pakistan, where the two-nation theory that was used to vivisect the subcontinent proved of immense assistance to Whitehall in the prolongation of British rule, both India as well as Indonesia have a history of standing up to colonial oppressors, and this and other links between the two countries have the potential to bring back to life the closeness between Jakarta and Delhi that was witnessed in the 1950s. In the contest between competing visions of the future, India needs to play a keystone role, but to do that, the country needs to 'lead by example' far more than is the case even to the present.

'Leading by example' should not imply appeasement of exclusivism. Among the reasons why there has been a growth of assertive manifestations of belief within the Hindu population is the neglect of historical justice by the Congress Party during and after the freedom struggle. Even a requisite as basic to religious rights as the restoration of the three holy sites of Hinduism (in Ayodhya, Kashi and Mathura) was not even attempted prior to the formation of the Modi government in 2014. The restoration of these three sites to what they were before being destroyed and built over by Aurangzeb (1618–1707) would have the effect of creating a firebreak that would act as a barrier to a drift by segments of the Hindu population towards exclusivist views. Mahatma Gandhi as well as his designated successor Prime Minister Jawaharlal Nehru concentrated on allaying the fears of being overwhelmed by the Hindu majority, but this was done by placating the radical and extremist fringe within the Muslim community rather than by empowering the moderate majority within the minority, as should have been the case. In a different context and not fully in an identical manner, the US made a similar error in the case of Afghanistan during the period of Soviet occupation in the 1980s by going along with the Pakistan military's policy of funding, training and equipping the Wahhabi fringe of the Pashtun population in Afghanistan rather than the moderates. In large part, this was out of fear that several Pashtun moderates, including those in Pakistan, had not abandoned hopes of forming an independent Pashtun state through unifying Pashtun-majority territories in Pakistan and Afghanistan. Backing the fringe while ignoring the moderate majority is never sound policy, and yet this is the path that has repeatedly been taken both domestically and externally by policymakers in the democracies.

A part of Asia that is overwhelmingly Muslim in composition is Central Asia. After the collapse of the USSR, the Sovietized school system followed in the Central Asian countries that emerged from the wreckage of the Soviet Union sought to replace their curricula, especially at the school level.

Unfortunately, petrodollar cash resulted in the replacement of Sovietized curricula with Wahhabi texts. This continued for nearly two decades, before the danger of radicalization of youths was acknowledged by policymakers, and changes were made. Unfortunately, since around 2015, there has been an effort at reviving Wahhabism within Central Asia as a consequence of the Chinese reliance on Pakistan (specifically its military) that has been a prominent part of the policies of General Secretary Xi. Rather than acting as a dampener, the PRC has acted as a force multiplier to GHQ Rawalpindi in the latter's propagation of the exclusivist and supremacist tenets wherever it has access to the policymaking process. The heft of the PRC within the Central Asian republics has boosted the capacity of Pakistan to renew earlier efforts by some Arab states to spread Wahhabism in the region. Should this succeed, parts of Central Asia would join parts of newly Taliban-led Afghanistan in serving as a base for terror groups looking to strike at democracies in Europe and Asia. Not only by extractive and mercantilist policies designed to raise its own level of economic performance without much care for the longer-term effect of its methods on the countries it is dealing with, but by its use by GHQ Rawalpindi as a force multiplier, the PRC under Xi may be at risk of emerging not simply as a disruptive but as a destructive force, and not just in Asia. Under Xi, a boost has been given to the activities of the Sino-Wahhabi lobby, even as he has strengthened the fabric of the Sino-Russian lobby.

8

Be Confused, Ambivalent or Decisive?
The Choice Facing Countries

In an age when androgyny has moved from not just being socially acceptable but increasingly desirable, it is not a surprise that several countries have sought to adopt a 'hedging' strategy. Through such a course, they either move in one direction or the other where external policy is concerned. Parallelly, they adopt a stance of support to (competing) sides that is often regarded by the countries being dealt with as not a sensible policy choice but a confused one, the nuances of which are often incomprehensible to the two sides sought to be straddled. Such a line of policy has usually been described as 'non-alignment'.

In actuality, the policy of 'non-alignment' first articulated by Prime Minister Jawaharlal Nehru and subsequently adopted by Presidents Gamal Abdel Nasser and Josip Broz Tito of Egypt and Yugoslavia, respectively, was in effect a choosing of sides without explicitly saying so. Both Nehru and Nasser leant towards the USSR while seeking to keep their lines of communication open, especially with the US, so as to avoid the blowback that an open identification with the Soviet Bloc would cause. In the case of Tito, he was wary of the manner in which the USSR wanted its allies to move in lockstep with it, while aware of the destructive potential of that country where his was concerned.

The 1967 war against the State of Israel that was launched by Egypt had no objective causes when looked at through the prism of Egypt's needs, but Nasser was fixated on uniting the Arab world and believed that defeating the Jewish state on the field of battle would establish his hold over the hearts and minds of the Arab world. Had the Egyptian forces and their Syrian and Jordanian allies prevailed, that may have happened, although even then not enough to bring down the structure of absolute princely rule and replace them with a republican or quasi-republican construct within the broader Arab world, in the manner President Nasser favoured. The victory of Israel in the 1967 conflict demolished the standing of Nasser and with it, the threat of republican and broadly secular pan-Arabism across the swathe of territory populated by that gifted people. Resistance to the supply of weapons from the USSR to Egypt together with the long-standing US policy of full backing for Israel meant that pan-Arabism and its corollary of Arab nationalism were regarded as anathema in Washington and within the councils of NATO. After the 1967 Egypt-Israel war, support for authoritarian Middle Eastern countries became a staple of the foreign policy of the Atlantic Alliance, whether they be ruled by royal families or by despots who went through the charade of holding elections with predetermined outcomes.

Whether it be the uncaring reaction of Prime Minister Nehru to the occupation of Hungary by Soviet troops in 1956 or a similar approach of Prime Minister Indira Gandhi to the 1968 crushing of Czechoslovakian resistance to the loss of sovereignty imposed through the Warsaw Pact, it was evident that non-alignment meant distance from the Atlantic Alliance without actually saying so. The reason why such a policy is being described as 'confused' is that it avoided a clear-cut affirmation of alliance with one of the two competing blocs during Cold War 1.0 between the USSR and the US, while in the effort to be 'non-aligned', on occasion stances favourable to Washington were taken by capitals such as Delhi and stands pleasing to Moscow were taken by Belgrade under Tito, who was loathe to accept Soviet overlordship over his country but unwilling to walk the extra distance so as to formally join the US-led alliance. As a consequence, Yugoslavia was deprived of the volume of US support received by countries such as France, Italy and (West) Germany while correctly regarded by the USSR as 'disloyal' (i.e., less than fully obedient) and treated as such. Tito was thereby prevented from building up the economy of his country sufficiently to ensure greater cohesion within its nationalities, a fate similar to India's during the full flowering of its non-alignment policy, when it began to lag behind several other Asian countries in economic and social parameters. Or to Egypt, even after Nasser's successor, Anwar al-Sadat, reversed the foreign and security policy of his predecessor and joined hands with the Atlantic Alliance, including with Israel, a change of course exemplified by the 1978 Camp David accords signed by President Sadat and Prime Minister Menachem Begin of Israel, among the benefits of which was the return of the Sinai to Egypt after it was seized by Israel in 1967. Begin followed a policy of ensuring 'peace through mutual concessions', a contrast to the stance now being adopted by Xi Jinping of the PRC, which is 'peace through unilateral concessions', which is defined to mean concessions made entirely by the other side.

It is a safe wager that neither the border agreement reached by the PRC with Myanmar in 1960 (and which could have been followed soon afterwards with a similar agreement with India, had the proposal of Premier Zhou

Enlai for a settlement on the basis of the then status quo not been rejected by Nehru) nor that signed between Beijing and Moscow in 1991 would have been possible had Xi been in charge of the CPC during those times. Not reading the lessons of the past, present or future is characteristic of the thinking of a 'confused' power, and it must be admitted that this unwelcome trait remains visible in at least some parts of the foreign and security policies of the Republic of India, not to mention economic ones, too.

A regional power of continental significance that may give an appearance of belonging to the 'confused' bracket is Vietnam, which has single-party rule under the Communist Party of Vietnam. The country continues to deal extensively with the PRC (and its ally the Russian Federation) while increasing its cooperation with the US. However, this policy is not the consequence of ambivalence (as is the case with India) but concentration on the overall course of action which (in the view of the Communist Party of Vietnam) is most favourable to a people who have endured considerable hardship to regain their freedom from colonial rule and later the unity of their country. The victory of the 'rag-tag' forces (a description given by the Atlantic Alliance) of General Vo Nguyen Giap over the French garrison in that redoubt in 1954 shattered the will of Paris to hold on to not just Vietnam but the rest of Indo-China, which was formally freed at the accord signed in Geneva that very year. It was only a partial victory for Ho Chi Minh, the founder of modern Vietnam, for the land south of the seventeenth parallel was handed over to a supporter of the French colonialists, Emperor Bao Dai.

As in earlier instances, the influence over US policy of the Atlantic Alliance resulted in Washington stepping into the role of overlord that had been vacated by Paris and taking over the fighting. In 1973, the US acknowledged the defeat of its militaries, although Vietnamese forces linked to it continued fighting till 1975, when the country was finally unified, and Saigon was renamed after Ho Chi Minh. In line with its policy of backing the US in its struggle to ensure the meltdown of the USSR, the PRC was less than enthusiastic about a unified Vietnam, especially under another nominally communist party, and invaded the country in 1979 'to teach Vietnam a lesson'. Instead, as took place in Finland in 1939–40, it was the PRC that was taught a lesson by the ferocious resistance of Vietnamese troops. In the earlier case, although the Finns got the worst of the encounter, the damage inflicted by them on the Red Army was considerable and boosted the confidence of Hitler that invasion of the USSR would be almost as smoothly successful a process as the invasion and occupation of France in 1940 had been. It helped the invaders that Stalin had been misled by planted disinformation from Berlin that several of his best generals were planning a putsch against him. This led the CPSU general secretary into ordering a culling of the officer ranks of the Red Army that reached fever pitch in 1937 and continued until the military setbacks subsequent to the invasion by the German military in 1941. This finally convinced Stalin of the lunacy of the purge and several of the surviving officers were brought back from gulags and given commands, while the culling slowed to a crawl and almost ceased during the remainder of the war against Germany. Among significant potential security risks in any country are intelligence officers who knowingly present dossiers that are known by them to be false, usually at the behest of the political leadership of the day or a foreign power. Aware of Stalin's paranoid instincts, the German security agencies boosted the number of Red Army senior officers about whom they planted false proof of collusion with themselves and with the Wehrmacht. The Soviet dictator took the bait left in his direction in its entirety and inflicted incalculable damage on the Soviet military by denuding it of several of its finest officers, individuals with the skill and experience to stand up to the Wehrmacht in combat that their replacements lacked.

Now that Cold War 2.0 has been acknowledged as a reality, even if this has been expressed in different terms by many world leaders, the centrality of an India-US pairing in taking on the Sino-Russian alliance is obvious. Thus far, the overhang of the past on policy in Delhi as well as in Washington has created a situation where progress in the relationship has been by fits and starts, often in a zigzag pattern where forward movement is followed by the reverse trajectory. An example was the incident involving a US warship passing through India's Exclusive Economic Zone in April 2020. This was followed by a statement from the Pentagon that India's claims over the extent of its exclusive waters were excessive, and it was to demonstrate the Pentagon's commitment to a 'free and open Indo-Pacific' that the warship had transited where it did. The public slap was met by a more sedate but disapproving response from the Ministry of External Affairs about the incident.

Treaty allies of the US and indeed most countries except for China do not usually make much of such transits by US warships. India joined China and Russia in its unease at the movement of a vessel that was part of the fleet of a Quad member. India had signed a treaty for mutual logistical support for each other in the movement of military assets, another reason why the sharp reaction was unexpected. Expectedly, the incident was used by lobbies opposed to the increasing congruence between the US and Indian militaries to revive past prejudices of the US being an 'unreliable' partner, not to mention efforts to revive the anger among the public at the news in 1971 that the US 7th fleet was closing in on India while the army of the world's most populous democracy was rescuing the people of Bangladesh from the Pakistan military's genocidal operations. In case the transit off the Lakshadweep islands was not a routine exercise and was intended to convey a message to the Indian side, it may have been a further reminder that going ahead with the purchase of S-400 missile systems from the Russian Federation would exact a price where US-India military ties were concerned. Washington, during Biden's presidency, accepts the centrality of co-opting India into an overall strategy to keep the Indo-Pacific from coming under the sway of the Sino-Russian alliance.[1] However, bits and pieces of policy left over from the Clinton era, in particular, appear to be complicating the process of engagement. An example was the March 2021 visit of US Defence Secretary Lloyd Austin to India (his first overseas tour since taking over). At the end of the trip, he made references to his having given lectures to his Indian counterparts on human rights issues, a seeming effort at propitiating India-phobes within the Democratic Party that was promptly controverted by the Indian side, to silence from the Pentagon.

Although the US sometimes appears contradictory in its interactions with India, it is not confused or ambivalent about the need to ensure the inclusion of Delhi in an alliance (by whatever name) that is designed to counter the progress towards primacy that is being made by China. In the case of India, its swings in policy from choices that reflect hope in

---

[1] Tara Kartha, 'In Declassified US' Secret Indo-Pacific Strategy, India Is Central, Pakistan Has Fallen Out', ThePrint, 18 January 2021, https://theprint.in/opinion/a-lot-has-changed-in-us-strategic-outlook-india-at-centre-of-plan-pakistan-has-fallen-out/587342/.

the PRC coming to its senses and appreciate the importance of friendly relations with what is currently the most populous country in the world to those that factor in the inevitability of a fundamental divergence of strategic interest between the two (at least so far as Beijing is concerned) has been confusing to its potential partners, including the US. In a way, such swings in the direction of policy are to be expected in a democracy, where competing lobbies battle each other in ensuring policy that meets their wishes. What seems to have been forgotten is that the time for such reflection may be over. General Secretary Xi has legitimized even the most extravagant territorial and other claims of the PRC. Xi has also indicated that in place of an indeterminate timetable for achieving these objectives, clearer and shorter timelines have been decided upon. The CPC general secretary has also placed the CMC and its narrower band of thinking at the heart of the policy formulation process, much as it took place in Japan during the 1930s. Institutions in India act as though time will never run out. For those at the business end of the big stick that is being developed and with rising frequency being wielded by Xi, time may be running out to cobble together an alliance that has both the capacity and the will to confront the challenge posed by a dispensation in Beijing that has both clarity and confidence in its 'manifest destiny' of the PRC prevailing over the US in the course of Cold War 2.0, just as the US prevailed over the USSR during Cold War 1.0.

India followed by Japan forms the keystone of the security architecture needed by the US to prevent the domination of the Indo-Pacific and its littoral states from the Sino-Russian alliance. Other vital members of such an alliance are Vietnam and Indonesia. India's reservoir of manpower proficient in warfare makes the country a necessary partner for the US in an Indo-Pacific security partnership. The addition of Australia and Japan is sufficient to enable a successful fightback against kinetic moves by adverse powers to dominate the Indo-Pacific. Additionally, if Indonesia, Vietnam and the Philippines were to be added to the forces unitedly defending freedom and ease of navigation in the Indo-Pacific as well as the maintenance of sovereignty by the countries in the region, the chances of a hostile force launching an attack would dwindle to a level close to insignificance. In the event of the creation of such an alliance being defensive and not offensive, the objective would be to deter adversaries from initiating a kinetic exchange or inflicting damage on the interests of other countries through non-kinetic warfare, as for example through the use of cyberspace. The primary PRC-created flashpoints in the Indo-Pacific are Taiwan, the South China Sea and the Himalayan massif, and the protection of each is necessary. In the case of the South China Sea, the expansive claims of the PRC to practically the whole of its waters need to be countered in a manner different from the past, when there was passive acceptance even of major changes to the status quo. These include:

(1) PLA occupation of small islands or the creation of artificial islands that were subsequently garrisoned by naval and other pickets.

(2) PRC blocking through coercive measures countries such as the Philippines and Vietnam from utilizing the resources of portions of the South China Sea (which may in future be renamed the ASEAN Sea).

(3) Regular patrols by elements of the PLA on sea and air in the South China Sea and warnings given to vessels and air assets nearby that they are 'in PRC territory', when the same is patently not the case.

(4) Seizure of islands belonging to other countries, such as the Scarborough Shoals from the Philippines, which till now has been met only with verbal objections even from countries such as the US that have long been formally committed to ensuring the security of the Philippines.

What the leadership of the PRC is attempting to achieve through the PLA is analogous to what the country has already achieved in much of the economic sphere, which is to ensure the transfer of entire lines of production to itself from other countries, including the US and India. Through its policy of adjusting the prices of items exported by it in such a way that domestic and other competition in the target country gets disadvantaged, and using the provisions of the World Trade Organization (WTO) to its advantage in a manner that other countries are unable to do in their markets, the PRC has become the manufactory of the world. Its control over the supply of intermediate and increasingly finished products has overtaken that of any other country, a situation that gives immense power to change the behaviour of countries through the commercial card. Now that primacy is giving way to a position of dominance in a growing number of supply chains, General Secretary Xi has focused also on achieving similar success in the conquest of territory in land, sea and space, and for this, the instrument chosen by him is the armoury of non-kinetic warfare systems possessed by the PRC as well as the similarly growing kinetic capability of the PLA. Now territory on sea and land is being sought by China just as the country absorbed so much manufacturing capability from other countries. The difference is that such a 'grab' is being regarded in a far less benign light than was the replacing by the PRC of the manufacturing capability of other countries.

The growing opposition to the expansionism of China is regarded in that country as a reflection of envy or the desire to prevent the world's second largest economy from overtaking the first. Attempts at territorial expansion have become commonplace so far as the policies of the PRC are concerned, but these are regarded as nothing more than China getting its due, getting justice in restitution for the 'century of humiliation' it has undergone in the past. The appetite for such 'restitution' appears to have become much more pronounced since 2012, the year when Xi Jinping took over as general secretary of the CPC, chairman of the CMC and president—his titles in descending order of importance. When a country convinces itself through its leadership that it is still a victim when the rest of the world has long been supportive of its impulse for economic growth, and it has not faced any conflict save those which it participated in or initiated, there is a propensity for actions that are unwarranted by objective circumstances but are the product of subjective estimates of how much punishment other countries will bear before reacting.

Should such a reaction be absent despite moves that are subjectively justified by the leadership while being objectively acts of coercion and aggression, such behaviour will only increase, with consequent side effects. Once the source of such behaviour by a country is understood to be motivated by subjective impulses (such as the 'right' of a particular 'race' to *Lebensraum* at the expense of other powers), delay in reaction designed to halt and subsequently reverse the effects of such behaviour by countries already affected and who are likely in future to be affected will not change such subjective impulses but strengthen them. Reason and fact are not the parameters within which policies framed by the subjective mind operate.

India and the US will have a mutually felt need to come closer because of the common threats of violence and terror-prone religious extremism and expansionary authoritarianism. So will Indonesia and India, especially in the context of the need for both to ensure that extremist logic does not emasculate moderate elements in society. The two countries together have around 40 per cent of the world's Muslim population, and working together across a range of fields would strengthen the moderate majority within these segments and shrink the appeal of the extremist fringe. This is made more important in view of the close working relationship that has been established over half a century between GHQ Rawalpindi (the Pakistan military) and its Chinese counterpart, the CMC of the CPC and the institution it controls, the PLA. Both militaries rely substantially on asymmetric methods of warfare, and assistance in logistics, equipment and much else from China has acted as a force multiplier for the Pakistan Army, which has long been much more successful in fighting in a non-conventional rather than in a conventional way. Seeking the weakening of resistance in an opponent before a kinetic attack has also been a standard procedure in PLA doctrine, and in such a context, the array of tactics and tools used by GHQ Rawalpindi is increasingly getting duplicated within its PRC counterpart, often through channels not directly linked to the military. The fusion in tactics between the Pakistan and Chinese militaries and the enhanced and specific risks posed to other powers by such collaboration mandate a close working relationship across spheres of national activity between Indonesia and India. The Philippines has, similar to India, lost territory to China and has substantial value as a partner in a network designed to ensure that further encroachments by the same source cease.

9

The Clash within and
between Continents

Even in groups of a few individuals, differences of opinion
and attitude occur that may lead to the use of force by one or
more of those involved. No wonder that units of continental
size carry multiple differences and differentiations within their
boundaries. Or that continents overall may have segments
of stress in their relationship with each other. An example is
Asia, a continent that less than a century ago was dominated
by countries located in Europe. It is almost amusing that to
many in that continent, especially those countries that have
in the past secured vast colonies, such as France, Spain and
Britain, the history of a former colony is treated as beginning
from the period when citizens of the colonizing country first
entered their future colony. History in India, for example, was
made (and substantially continues) to place emphasis on the
period of colonial rule, while the past was rendered as more and
more indistinct and opaque the further back the recital went.
The 'natives' learning such histories faced the risk of losing
appreciation and knowledge of their societal roots, in effect
looking at themselves as having cultural DNA that had almost
been 'created' by the occupying power.

So deep was the perception of dependency that after India won its freedom from British rule on 15 August 1947, the leaders of the newly independent country beseeched the outgoing British viceroy, Lord Louis Mountbatten, to continue as the first governor general of independent India. In Africa, several countries that had once been the colonies of France have as their leaders individuals who consider France the 'mother country', just as several among the elite in Mexico refer to visits to Spain as 'going home'. As for the US, where every human being is deemed by the constitution itself to be created equal to any other, the history of that country has been arbitrarily and inaccurately placed as beginning from the period of occupation by settlers from the British Isles. As in the countries of South America, serious efforts at retrieval of the immense store of cultural and other treasures of societies as they existed prior to conquest by the Europeans have only recently been placed on a faster track. A people deprived of knowledge of the wonders of their past are at risk of being handicapped through an inner lack of confidence in themselves in their pursuit of an equal future. That the people of India have a better level of awareness of the past of their land and its civilization (albeit secured through ways other than in school or university) may be a factor in the global success of the Indian diaspora, especially in those countries that are more enlightened in the latitude they give to those who are residents or citizens settling from afar.

Just as has taken place in Asia over the past century, interest in and awareness of the pre-colonial past has shown a substantial increase in Africa and South America, where for a considerable period, the elites sought to 'Europeanize' themselves in different ways, including by frequent visits to the 'mother civilization'. In the process, their real 'mother' (the pre-colonial civilization of their own land and people) was neglected if not completely ignored. Human society is not 'vertical' but 'horizontal', in that diverse societies are neither 'inferior' nor 'superior' to any other, merely different but essentially equal. Religions sought to emphasize this, as for example the Christian claim that the entirety of humanity, all seven billion and more on earth, come from Adam and Eve. Ancient tradition in India places immense value on the concept of '*Vasudhaiva Kutumbakam*', that the entire world is one family. The Quran confers on every believer the right to independently reach out to the message contained in its verses, irrespective of social or ethnic origin. Even those who do not accept the central pillar of the faith (that there is but one almighty and Muhammad is the messenger) are acknowledged to be offspring of the same almighty and are therefore brothers and sisters to each other. Unfortunately, in almost all faiths, interpreters (usually from within the priesthood) have sought to give their own characterization of the theology of a faith rather than themselves obey the tenet that every individual has the right and the wisdom needed to reach his or her own understanding of the catechism.

It was not accidental that those countries made the most progress where the rights and freedoms of the citizen were protected, and where the boundaries of both expanded. The PRC, which during the final years of the twentieth century emerged as the alternative superpower to the US after the collapse of the USSR in 1992, is considered as having disproved any link between individual freedom and economic progress. The reality is that the evolution of its governance mechanism since the onset of the Deng Xiaoping era in the 1980s transferred substantial degrees of freedom from the state to the citizen. This was visible in the economic sphere, although even societally, behaviour patterns reflected personal freedoms that were not present even during the period in between imperial rule and the founding of the PRC by Mao Zedong in 1949. The jury is still out on the eventual effect of the restrictions in many such freedoms that have been brought into place with the takeover as general secretary of the Party by Xi in 2012. Taking a people forward societally and economically is, after all, an entirely different situation than dragging them backwards, of course always in the name of a 'higher' purpose.

Even in India, a country where democracy has travelled a considerable distance when compared with several other states in Asia, Africa and South America, after Independence in 1947, it took until 2014 before Narendra Damodardas Modi, a leader from the 'other backward classes', took over as the prime minister of the country. Till then, that keystone position within the governance system was held by those from the 'forward castes', and for most of the time, by those belonging to the Brahmin community, which in the somewhat irrational hierarchy of 'caste by birth' is considered the highest within that set of classifications. Similarly, whether it be in Mexico, a country that has gone through several social upheavals seemingly designed to raise the level of the underprivileged, almost all its leaders have come from the tiny sliver of the population that has substantially been Europeanized, or in more precise language, adopted the mores and affectations of Spanish society. Brazil is a country where the Europeanized segment still dominates business and politics. Portuguese influence is much less than Spanish influence in Mexico as the country has attracted settlers from across Europe, including from Italy and Germany. Because of its past as a colony of Portugal rather than Spain, and the language of the former being the lingua franca rather than that of the latter, a linguistic fault line has been created that has reduced the influence of Brazil over the rest of the continent to a level much below that which its size and potential entitles it to. Except in North America, where there remains no ambiguity over which is the primary power, in no other continent has a single country been able to secure dominance or at the least primacy over the rest, although the PRC has been working at this for some time in Asia and since the 1990s, in Africa.

Two concepts were among those elucidated by the present writer in his previous writings. These were the concept of a twenty-first-century Anglosphere (where the factor of ethnicity was considered central previously but has been replaced with language), or the increasing acceptance within the social sciences that human societies need to be seen as 'horizontal' (different but equal) rather than 'vertical' (separate and unequal). Such a view has increased traction for studies of societies, particularly in countries that had long defined their identities as belonging only to the period since they were inhabited by those of European extraction or in the case of Tibet, Xinjiang, Manchuria and Inner Mongolia, now part of the PRC, from the period when elements of the Han population took control in them. Previous periods were characterized as undesirable, this put down in a manner as clear as was possible for those writing such 'new' histories to attempt.

As the lessons and teachings being retrieved from Native American civilization prove, much that is valuable and relevant to this day (such as the focus on a sustainable planet) was contained in those civilizations and peoples that were overwhelmed by others, and in many cases, sharply reduced in size. In South America, an adverse reaction to the self-absorption of the Europeanized elite among the majority of the population has led to the coming to office of leaders who are not from that elite either in terms of wealth or ethnicity. The reading of history has become more nuanced and reflective of the entire history of a country and its peoples rather than simply a recital of the 'glorious era' when those who colonized the land and the people there arrived on its boundaries, with the period before being presented as an 'area of darkness', to borrow a phrase used in the title of a book by V.S. Naipaul. A darkness in which nothing is visible.

In the ongoing contest for primacy between the PRC and the US, the latter has been assisted in the 'soft power' aspect by the fact of it having a medley of peoples and cultures rather than being dominated by a single denomination in the manner that the Han population does in the PRC. There is discomfort among a section of the majority ('white') population of the US, especially at the self-assertion of the African American community, which led to the election of Donald John Trump as the 45th President of the US in 2016. The manner in which Trump sought to shield the majority status of the 'white' community by various moves designed to prevent entry of, or to lower the political influence of, the 'non-white' population has been recorded. Trump's term in the White House led to the election of Joe Biden in 2020 because of a reaction even within the 'white' community, which is substantially composed of elements who do not share Trump adviser Stephen Miller's evident distaste for those who are 'non-white'.

The attempted panacea of encouraging migration of 'whites' into the US while discouraging the rest makes no sense in a world increasingly made 'flat' by technology and education. Or, indeed, by the rise of Asia, a continent that is almost entirely 'non-white'. A war of ethnicities is as harmful to society as a war over religion, and it must be added that such a lesson was not always grasped by (for example) leaders in parts of South America who came to power because of political assertion of the non-Europeanized segments of the population.

The discrimination of the past was sought to be replaced with reverse discrimination against those who had earlier formed the ruling class. A similar situation prevailed in some parts of Africa, notably in Zimbabwe under Robert Mugabe. Unsurprisingly, the more tolerant societies in both continents grew faster and in a stabler way than the others. Discrimination in the past by the elite resulted in the enrichment of a small number and the impoverishment of the rest. A similar level of expropriatory discrimination against the small minority that comprises the elite is usually not the most effective pathway towards reducing poverty among most of the population. Just as a 'public private partnership' between the government and the private sector often delivers results that are much more pronounced than if either were to attempt a task alone, an amicable accommodation between the resources of the elite and the capacities of the less privileged majority may be the best solution. Of course, as Alfred Marshall wrote in his *Principles of Economics*, the 'Residuum', the poorer sections of society, needed to be given a leg-up for equity as well as societal stability. A satisfactory economic policy mix (with an accompanying foreign policy) would enable the middle class to grow through an acceleration of entry of the 'lower' classes into it, even as each year a proportion of the middle class graduates to the level of the elite.

An economy in which the middle class shrinks through more and more from that group entering not the elite, but the 'lower' classes, will generate societal pressures that may result in eruptions of unrest and even mob violence that would finally affect even the lives of the elite. An increase in the number of billionaires in a country need not be an indicator of societal or economic health, unless more and more of them have graduated from the middle class even as the number of that group grows through the entry of those moving upwards from the 'lower' classes. The more such upward progress, the better the prospects for sustained growth and stability. Geopolitical factors as well as 'smart' policies may result in some continents becoming wealthier than others, or some countries in a particular continent making more progress than the rest. As more than a few economists have pointed out, the greater the dissemination of prosperity within the entire population of a country, the stronger will be its capacity to absorb shocks such as an armed invasion by a foreign power or the spread of a pandemic.

In a world where the 'sanctions toolkit' is resorted to, including by the PRC albeit in a less comprehensive way than the US for instance, the greater the monopoly of the elite in the formulation of policy, the lower will be the 'change of policy' effect caused through sanctions, unless these target not an entire country but only a set of individuals responsible for taking the decisions that the sanctioning country regards as unacceptable. Sanctions, if imposed, need to be routed in the manner of a sniper's bullet, rather than the spray that comes from an automatic weapon firing indiscriminately. Given that the overwhelming majority of the population of most countries that are the target of sanctions by the PRC, the US and within the EU (the three who most indulge in this practice) are innocent of any role in the policy process, such 'automatic fire' sanctions merely give a pathway to the elite to transfer the responsibility for worsening of already bad conditions to the sanctioning countries. In this way, sanctions may result in strengthening the grip of elites over policy rather than weakening them, as was seen in Iraq under Saddam Hussein.

Policy emerging from the Lutyens Zone has kept India in a situation in which the country experiences most of the shocks of adverse geopolitical conditions while gaining negligible advantage from geopolitical tailwinds. Such ambivalence, born essentially from the lack of clarity in the identification of threats and opportunities, has been passed off as 'strategic ambiguity' or even 'strategic independence' (defined in practice as the freedom to miss out on opportunities that could benefit the country). India is not the only country in such a group. There are several, such as many of the countries of Asia, Africa and South America, who appear to oscillate in the manner of hummingbirds between the US and the PRC.

The methodical way the PRC has sought to control the global supply chains has resulted in its long-standing status as the default option for investors looking beyond their home countries. However, the embedding of tech within an increasing share of product, and the ability of tech to funnel information that may be useful in times of war or subversion, has resulted in a steady decoupling of multiple supply chains from China. Or in the case of the PRC (and the Russian Federation), from the US. Given the intensification of Sino-US rivalry and the need for either superpower to ensure that data relevant to the other side in planning a covert or overt attack by the other, rather than the ten to fifteen years that has been postulated as being the time frame for the hi-tech decoupling process to be largely complete, three to five years seems a more likely estimate. Among the beneficiaries of the transfer of productive assets from the PRC to locations close to the US and its allies could be India, assuming that Prime Minister Modi is not deflected from continuing with some of the policy reforms that he has initiated during his second term (2019–24).

Cold War 2.0 became inevitable during the second term of CPC General Secretary Hu Jintao, when the 2008 (Wall Street-created) global financial collapse emboldened the inner councils of the CPC into believing that the time when Beijing would eclipse Washington as the primary hub of geopolitical significance was no longer indeterminate, but was close at hand.[1] Thus far, although the PRC had by then hollowed out significant chunks of manufacturing capability from several major economies, it was not seen by the Atlantic Alliance as posing anywhere close to an immediate threat to the supremacy of the US in both the Indo-Pacific as well as in the Atlantic. Such a switch was sought to be accelerated significantly by incoming General Secretary Xi. By 2015, the PRC had outpaced the US and the EU in several fields related to advanced technology and was closing in on the others. The PLA-focused Xi paid particular attention to Artificial Intelligence and was fortunate in having the benefit of a cadre of technologists and scientists animated by the goal of global primacy of the CPC leadership. Once enterprises in the PRC began to be proficient in the technology and scientific fields that the Atlantic Alliance had regarded as their monopoly, it became apparent to an increasing number of policymakers on both sides of the Atlantic that either they would have to soon adjust to a world where Beijing and its 'Chinese communist' system was numero uno or begin to work to constrain the PRC. Only such an effort could result in a deceleration in the PRC's progress towards replacing the Atlantic Alliance as the natural incubator of constantly improving technologies.

Whether through securing such knowledge through means other than what was public or by the patriotic dedication

---

[1] Niall Ferguson in Srijana Mitra Das, 'We're in Cold War 2—China Is the Soviet Union's Heir. India under PM Modi Is Very Close to the USA', *Times of India*, September 28, 2020, https://timesofindia.indiatimes.com/world/rest-of-world/we-are-in-cold-war-2-now-and-china-is-the-heir-of-soviet-union/articleshow/78355934.cms.

instilled in several citizens of the PRC (as well as a segment of Overseas Chinese), the speed with which China was catching up with the US in practical outcomes, rendered possible by advanced research, had come within full public view across the world by 2017. From that time onwards, just as countries in Africa, Asia and South America had a systemic and diplomatic option in the USSR rather than follow the lead given by the US, such countries finally had after the Soviet Union self-destructed in 1992 an alternative to the US in the PRC, which had more than a decade prior to 2017 evolved into a superpower. Unlike the US, where talent was welcomed (until recently even from China) in order to generate new technologies, the PRC has kept its advanced research and development a closed shop, using and trusting only its own people.

The replacement suggested by the PRC to the 'Washington Consensus' is of course the 'Beijing Consensus', which is helpfully imprecise on points other than the central tenet, which means—what is good for China is *ipso facto* good for the rest of the world. While Washington was emphatic that countries hewing to its dictates needed to declare such an affinity clearly and publicly, Beijing was satisfied if a country did what was regarded by the CPC leadership as convenient for the PRC, even if in public that country did not acknowledge any such fealty to China. This has enabled several countries to continue to behave in public as though they are linked to the US-led alliance while in effect working for the other side in several matters of significance to both the superpowers. Not just within continents but within multi-state groupings such as the EU, the South Asian Association for Regional Cooperation (SAARC) and the ASEAN, the PRC has succeeded in carving out its own zones of influence. This comprises both open support for the Beijing Consensus as also effective albeit covert backing that reveals itself only on the occasions when an open stand needs to be taken by a particular grouping of countries on a matter of importance relating to China. Demonstratively since the ascent of Xi to the top leadership of the CPC, Chinese diplomats have been active in every continent in their effort at ensuring that a country would, if not always back the PRC, remain (in terms of practical as distinct from verbal effect) neutral in disputes of significance that erupt between Beijing and Washington.

The worldwide dissemination of PRC-produced or -controlled data-gathering devices such as smartphones or apps has given Chinese diplomats (and soldiers) information on not just influential individuals in target countries but entire or swathes of populations within them. The prevalence of online gaming apps that generate user data, which flows to China, has assisted in forming a picture of the young within a population. What messages or stimuli make them joyful or unhappy and angry? Such information would assist in the use of social media platforms in different countries to generate opinions that are favourable to the Chinese point of view. Ideally, that are also unfavourable to governments regarded as obstructive even if not always hostile to the achievement of the objectives set by the PRC leadership. The across-the-board collation of information and consultation on tactics to be used is meant to ensure success in a possible kinetic and non-kinetic hostile operation by China against a target country. The weaknesses in the PRC system of governance are the lack of flexibility to react to unforeseen changes in circumstances or reactions, in view of the cumbersome nature of the collaborative process through which tactics get finalized. And often to a misreading of the individual(s) or situation(s) despite such an elaborate procedure. Of course, under Xi, the collaborative process has been shortened by reducing the number of layers and

individuals consulted before a decision gets taken at the
higher levels.

In the North American continent, Mexico is regarded
as the outlier, different from the US and Canada. However,
demographic trends in the US have increased the salience of its
southern neighbour, and the growth of the Latino community
in the US added to a steady increase in the wealth and education
of those on the other side of the Rio Grande have the effect of
bringing Mexico and the US together. There has been discussion
about the Spanish-speaking country serving as a bridge to other
countries in South America, except that Mexico is an outlier
not just to its north but to its south as well.

The other outlier in this continent, this time caused less
by culture and history than by language, is Brazil. While
the remainder of South America hardly seems united, the
development of a consciousness of history and culture among
the 'indigenous' or mainly indigenous populations of the
continent is likely to have the effect of knitting it closer together
than has been the case thus far, despite the efforts of leaders such
as Simon Bolivar. The domination of the Europeanized elite
in South America was not duplicated in India. Had a similar
phenomenon taken root there, the numerically small Anglo-
Indian community would have emerged as the upper layer of
post-colonial society. Instead, the community continued on the
fringe, with several migrating to Australia and the UK rather
than remaining behind in India.

The assertion of indigenous identity, once matched by
unequal opportunities in education and job placement in
countries such as Argentina and Chile, is likely to be a factor
that assists in the influence of India in the continent. Such
an outcome may be combined with the increasing levels of
multicultural participation in US politics and governance.

The Trump interlude was less a trend than a throwback that demographic changes and an increasing adaptation to multi-ethnic society within the white community in the US is going to make impossible to repeat after two more presidential election cycles in that country. Such a change in the mindset and attitudes of the white majority better enables Washington to build stronger understandings with countries in South America, Africa and Asia. Both Barack Obama as US president and Rishi Sunak as UK prime minister owed their success mainly to support within their 'white' electorates—in the Sunak case, Conservative Party MPs. This is a welcome shift from the attitude of successive US administrations that, thanks to the mindset caused by its centrality in the Atlantic Alliance, long acted as though it was only both the shores of the North Atlantic Ocean which defined its society. In reality, the US is a quadri-continental country, with influences permeating not just from Europe but from continents such as Africa, South America and Asia. This has the potential to provide substantial tailwind to its 'soft power' influence. As for its competitor in the global geopolitical sweepstakes, the PRC, the policy adopted by the world's other superpower has been to establish friendly and functional relationships with whichever elite is in charge of a country at any point in time. The PRC has no favourites except itself. Within its society, there is no question but that the Han are in charge.

While there will be initial setbacks to European diplomacy and influence as a consequence of the weakening hold of Europeanized segments in South America (and Mexico), this will be temporary. Europe is changing as well, although quirks in its immigration policies have led to migration from the Middle East and North African countries often initiated by violent turmoil. The skewed in the composition of migrants into the EU caused by this surge from a particular segment of the world's population has the potential to cause fissures to emerge in the future, as the young among those who relocated to the EU from the Middle East and North Africa become adult and have more children. It remains to be seen whether the experiment being tried out by President Macron of France to ensure that the cultural foundation of every French citizen (irrespective of faith or ethnicity) has a broad degree of uniformity based on the values of the republic. A development favourable to such an integration is the fightback against Wahhabism in several Muslim-majority countries, including the KSA. Success in this battle is vital not just to Asia and North Africa but to much of Europe as well, including Germany and Italy. Educational methods have the potential to be accessible to entire populations that was not possible in the past, and this technology-driven change is having an impact, especially in Africa. The continent is finally standing on the cusp of realization of its immense potential for the benefit of its own people, held back (as so many other countries are) only by angularities in the structure of governance and in the composition of those who operate such systems.

Just as it took place in Europe four centuries ago, technology is reaching the homes of 'ordinary' people in poorer countries, and more and more of the young are finding their lives changed as a consequence. Whether it is tele-medicine or tele-education, low-cost solutions are possible even as a few providers seek to encash through overpricing the temporary monopoly some of them have in specific locations over such methods.

Despite issues relating to tribal identity that bedevil not just the relationship between countries but that between communities in particular countries, Africa retains the potential to unite on issues of concern in a manner that the countries of Asia and South America have not succeeded in doing. The cleavage between the mainly French and English-speaking countries in Africa is getting narrower, not least because increasing numbers of the former are picking up a working knowledge of the international link language. Of course, not very far away is the widespread use of technologies that enable effortless (if not perfect) translation from one language to the other. Just as the Industrial Revolution changed the lives of people across both sides of the Atlantic in the eighteenth century, the Technology Revolution of the twenty-first century will transform lives across the world in a generation. The centrality of technology in everyday lives of almost the global population is of concern to the US, which is at risk of losing its dominance in the field to China. A necessary step in the constraining of the PRC from getting out of hand in its military adventures has been the technology transfer curbs imposed in 2022 by President Biden. These have gone far beyond the tariff measures put in place by his predecessor and are designed to ensure that Chinese tech gets fewer opportunities to piggyback on US tech in the manner it has since the 1980s.

10

Countries Navigate the Superpower Divide

When it comes to married couples, their friends usually try to be close to both the people involved. Should there be an acrimonious parting, many may be forced to choose between one former partner or the other, as being friendly to one may be viewed with disfavour by the other. In 1941, thanks to the wisdom shown by President Franklin D. Roosevelt and Prime Minister Churchill, there was a coming together of the USSR, the UK and the US after the former was attacked by Hitlerite Germany during the 1939–45 war. Soon after the close of that war, there was a clash between the objectives subsequently pursued by the USSR and the US. Both wanted to increase the list of countries that would be counted in their supporters' columns. The only country competing with the US in Europe (and shortly thereafter, in much of the rest of the world) was the Soviet Union, then still led by Marshal Stalin. To this day, just as the PRC is wary of an ascendant India for fear that Delhi could replace Beijing as the primary power in Asia, the US seeks to hobble Russia out of concern that an empowered Moscow could replace Washington as the driving force behind much of the security policy within the European Union.

In 1948, the Berlin Blockade imposed by Stalin strengthened the 'Containment' lobby in Washington at the expense of those who sought an accommodation with Moscow as a continuation of the partnership established during the world war that had just ended. Given the differences in governance systems and strategic objectives, that may have been an objective impossible to realize in the absence of significant concessions that a US administration would find it almost impossible to make.

Soon afterward the Berlin Blockade ended after Stalin blinked and both Moscow as well as Washington began reading from the same playbook. The content of this was best expressed by US President Bush after the 11 September 2001 terror attack, that countries were either with the US or against, that there was no longer room for neutrality. Choosing sides became an inevitability soon after the onset of Cold War 1.0 between the USSR and the US, with the latter in effect regarding those who opted for some form of neutrality as closet backers of the Soviet Union. Among the beneficiaries of the USSR-US Cold War were Pakistan in the 1950s and PRC in the 1970s. They first joined the numerous security-related organizations floated by Washington to 'contain communism'. The Eisenhower administration sought to make the point to India that the consequences of the neutrality embodied in Jawaharlal Nehru's doctrine of non-alignment would be unhelpful for India's future, and particularly so for any enhanced relationship with the US. The entry of Pakistan into US-crafted security groupings resulted in the US ignoring the growing cosiness between Pakistan and a formidable communist power, the PRC in the 1960s. This may have been because the largesse by the US to Pakistan was not intended to confront China but because of Pakistan's value as a source of trouble for neutralist (i.e., by Dullesian definition, pro-Soviet) India. Such an apparent motive on the part of its great benefactor was not a factor that would have persuaded the military rulers of Pakistan in particular to reverse their hostility towards the country that they had until 1947 been a part of.

Among the reasons why post-1947 India became a laggard in per capita terms when contrasted with US-aligned countries in East and Southeast Asia was the lack of flexibility in Atlanticist responses that was caused by the doctrine of non-alignment. The policy resulted in the Atlantic powers shifting to Pakistan's corner and making them champion that country's demand for further territorial concessions by India. This left little option for the Government of India but to move closer to the USSR, including in several measures relating to economic policy. Such a trend in policy was reinforced during the 1960s, when relations between Beijing and Delhi soured after His Holiness the 14th Dalai Lama of Tibet moved to India from Tibet, followed by the Sino-Indian 1962 border war.

At the same time, 'fraternal ties' between Beijing and Moscow soon developed into a somewhat less friendly form. It may be true that Prime Minister Jawaharlal Nehru passed up on most of the opportunities that India had to take advantage of western goodwill through adjusting economic and diplomatic policies. However, it is understandable that Nehru's personal experience of European colonialism may have predisposed him against working more closely with European powers, who were at the time still trying to retain control over several of their colonies rather than accepting the spirit of the times and handing over charge to the people of the countries they had ruled in an expropriatory fashion. As for the US, with the death of President Franklin D. Roosevelt in 1945, Washington reverted to its default policy of backing its European allies, even in some of their colonial adventures, as for example in Vietnam.

It was during the 1939–45 war that the US emerged as the head of the Atlantic Alliance. With the passing of President Roosevelt and the occupation of the White House by Harry S. Truman, a policy of backing the Atlantic Alliance partners was followed, whether in Asia or elsewhere. Uncritical support to European powers was the norm, although with rare exceptions such as over the 1956 Suez Crisis between the UK, France and Israel against Egypt. This was often at the cost of longer-term US interests and indeed the interests of those European countries who refused to accept the inevitability by then of a world devoid of colonialism, a world of the kind sought by Nehru, Nkrumah, Sukarno, Kenyatta and other African and Asian leaders who had succeeded in taking control of their countries from a European colonial power. Had there been greater understanding within Atlantic Alliance capitals of the reasons why Prime Minister Nehru refused to join the Cold War 1.0 security alliances crafted by the Atlantic powers, the coming into being by the close of the 1960s of a tacit Indo-Soviet alliance (which was formalized in 1971 with the signing of the Indo-Soviet treaty) may have been avoided, as would have been the nurturing of a military-controlled Pakistan into an academy for generating and training terror groups. These began to operate first in India and Afghanistan, then spread to Iran, and in the twenty-first century across the world. Until this point, their growth was ignored by the NATO members, especially the US and the UK, the country that had created Pakistan on explicitly religious grounds, and where both the Labour as well as the Conservative Party continue to retain a soft spot for that country, despite incidents of terror facilitated by the direct and indirect involvement of the Pakistan military.

Although neutral in official proclamations and less by its own design than by the flow of global events, India was considered even within that grouping to be a 'soft' member of the Soviet bloc. Such a situation may have been reversed had either Lal Bahadur Shastri or Morarji Desai been given more time than they were given in the South Block office of the prime minister of India. Efforts were made by President Ronald Reagan to woo Prime Minister Indira Gandhi away from 'non-alignment' in 1982. Some of the overreaction by President Jimmy Carter once in office to India's 'peaceful nuclear explosion' (PNE) in 1974 was walked back from. Had the 1974 PNE been followed up with more such experiments designed to improve the quality of the nuclear weapons tested, Washington may have been more respectful of India.

As it happened, as indeed it so often happened, the Government of India's ambivalent and contradictory policies led to India getting the worst of both the worlds. Neither did India secure the admittedly skimpy benefits of being in the Nuclear Non-Proliferation Treaty (NPT) nor the benefit of using such an exclusion to launch a robust programme designed to build a nuclear arsenal, in the manner that the leadership of China had earlier succeeded in doing. Its half steps ensured that while the PRC, with India's consistent support even in the midst of the 1962 war, was admitted into the more exclusive clubs within the international order, such as the permanent membership of the UN Security Council or joining the NPT as a formally acknowledged nuclear weapons state (together with the US, the USSR, Britain and France), India remained outside such clubs and continues to do so despite its size and potential. In substantial part, such a lack of formal acceptance of its position within the international order owes its origins to the ability of policymakers in India to so often displease every major external constituency, usually by seeking to placate each of them through piecemeal and mutually contradictory concessions.

Another reason is the avoidance in practice of acting in sync with the emphatic language frequently used by its officials to define India's stand. An example is the global war on terror, in which India had long been a bystander in every theatre except within the country, or in its immediate backyard. This is despite the significant manpower assets that the country with trained and experienced in counter-terrorism operations. A defensive mentality has long hung over the Lutyens Zone in Delhi that has resulted in verbal assertions not being matched by performance. There has been a propensity to draw lessons from experience in a manner that results in conclusions which fail to take account of policy lapses that converted success into disaster. The 1987–90 Indian Peacekeeping Force (IPKF) in Sri Lanka has been the usual excuse of those anxious to prevent the involvement of the military in external operations, and was used for example in 2003, when the US suggested that a division of 18,000 men from the Indian Army be stationed in the Kurdish region of Iraq. The fact is that the IPKF, despite its success in tackling the Liberation Tigers of Tamil Eelam (LTTE), was put on the defensive once the India-phobic Ranasinghe Premadasa was appointed President of Sri Lanka in January 1989. From the start, the new head of government opposed the presence of the IPKF in Sri Lanka, and covertly ensured that weapons and other assistance were supplied through him to the LTTE to help them fight the IPKF. When V.P. Singh took over from Rajiv Gandhi as prime minister of India in December 1989, he wasted no time in accepting Sri Lankan President Premadasa's insistent and suicidal requests that the IPKF leave his country, a request that V.P. Singh soon complied with in a manner reminiscent of President Biden's scurrying away from Afghanistan by August 2021.

The LTTE repaid President Premadasa for this life-saving favour by assassinating him in 1993, but errors in analysis drawn from the IPKF experience have so affected the policymaking community in India that external military involvement has been off the table since that time, despite the changes that have taken place within the Indian military since the 1980s. More than the habitual ambivalence of the policy establishment in India, it is the change in the public mood about the threat posed by Xi's China that is making inevitable the slow but steady movement of India in the strategic direction already taken by the other three members of the Quad (Japan, Australia and the US).

India is a necessary but not sufficient element in the protective chain that is being formed, and which has the Quad at its core. This formation is designed to prevent the hegemony of any single power over the Indo-Pacific. Such a situation would bring with it major consequences to the internal governance structure, society and economies of the littoral states of the Indo-Pacific. Under the Communist Party, China has over the years created an economic, political and societal system very different from that of the democracies. At the same time, its expansive ambitions are at variance with the countries around it. Such a list includes not only India but Vietnam as well, despite these countries' strong military capabilities. Despite the enervating effects of lingering influence within the portals of governance of the colonial past, crises that were unmanageable unless substantial reforms got carried out have in the past led to such reforms, such as in 1992 and 2020. In a similar way, despite the ambivalence and lack of clear direction in a part of the country's strategic and foreign policy, India is on track to join the other three Quad members (Japan, the US and Australia) to defend the Indo-Pacific against authoritarian expansion. Such a response has become necessary following the trajectory of Beijing in the Eurasian continent and in the Indo-Pacific.

In Africa, the very quantum of investments made by the PRC and the consequent debts incurred are likely to lead to the majority of the countries locating there choosing the Quad partners rather than the Sino-Russian alliance as the partnership to best meet twenty-first-century needs. A robust defence against authoritarian expansionism will build up the credibility of the Quad Plus (which needs to include Vietnam, France, the UK, the Philippines and Indonesia as well) sufficiently to enable countries in Asia, South America and Africa—that have been dragged into unsustainable levels of debt by the PRC—to repudiate such claims without the risk of becoming the target of armed attack by the PRC or surrendering their sovereign rights under a barrage of punitive actions that may be imposed by Beijing in order to suffocate the economy of any country that refuses to honour debt owed to the PRC. The world has seen during 2022 in Sri Lanka that the PRC is a moneylender who shows no mercy towards debtors, no matter how severe the impact of such debt on ordinary people. Another alternative to complete repudiation of debt owed to PRC entities would be to insist on repayment schedules that are affordable, such as zero payment for the first five years and repayment of the loan over the next fifty years at nominal interest. The repayment would be made not in USD or Renminbi (RMB, also known as Yuan) but in the currency of the debtor country at the value vis-à-vis the RMB when the debt to PRC entities was incurred. It would be a given that countries rescheduling or repudiating debt owed to the PRC would not face any adverse consequences from countries on the other side of the Great Divide caused by the onset of Cold War 2.0. Of course, such countries would need to choose their strategic direction: Are they with those favouring a free, open and inclusive Indo-Pacific or with the aspiring hegemon that has enmeshed them in debt and travail?

Had Trump continued as president of the United States for a second term, it may have been easier for the Sino-Russian alliance to win over more countries in South America and Africa to its side. Trump conducted much of his diplomacy in a manner that alienated the population at large if not always the elite in several countries from the White House. In contrast, the Biden-Harris administration has been more liberal in its approach to several countries. A problem would arise were President Biden's generosity and outreach towards the underprivileged applied only to citizens of his own country plus the Ukrainians, much as Prime Minister Churchill's commitment to freedom of the individual and absence of autocracy in governance applied only to those of European extraction. The Marshall Plan benefited the US at least as much as it did its beneficiaries in Europe. A similar show of US generosity towards countries that are geopolitically relevant despite having low per capita incomes may cause a similar effect. India, Brazil, South Africa and Indonesia are obvious examples of such countries. While Washington looks with disfavour on the Indian purchase of S-400 defensive systems from Russia, it has yet to offer the obvious alternative of installing and jointly operating a THAAD system in a location such as the Andaman Island chain. President Biden's open-handed generosity to Ukraine compares with an insistence to squeeze out as much money as possible from weapons sales to Taiwan and India, despite the threat being faced by Taipei and Delhi from the PRC, a country that is far more significant a threat than Russia. It would be unfair to impute racial motives to such a show of partiality by the White House, although it is clear that Taiwan (not to mention India) is far more important to overall US security than Ukraine, given that the theatre of most significance is no longer Europe but Asia, no longer the Atlantic but the Indo-Pacific.

Whether it be in Asia, Africa or in South America, the flattening of the curve of educational opportunity to the underprivileged through technology is essential. Such a transformation would result in an assertion of the right of public opinion to be given a seat at the table when policies concerning the people are being formulated. As a consequence of the expenditure on societal needs, the much greater understanding and sensitivity shown by the Biden-Harris administration towards the underprivileged in their country has been on display. The fiscal magnitude of the measures sought to be taken by President Biden, once effectively negotiated through the US Congress and implemented in the spirit in which they have been framed, could ensure for the 46th President of the US the level of popular support that was enjoyed by the 32nd President of the US, Roosevelt, towards the latter period of the 1930s.

Such a change in the public mood within the US would give the Biden-Harris team the cushion needed to innovate foreign policy, as Barack Obama did in the latter period of his stint in the White House. It was not the unpopularity of Obama but the unpopularity of the Democratic Party nominee for the presidency in 2016 that cost the party the White House. Somehow the perception that the Clintons have a sense of entitlement has affected their standing among the public in a country where politicians are expected to retain the common touch.

The Temer and Bolsonaro interludes may appear to disprove such a conclusion, but across Brazil as well as in several other countries in South America, pride in traditions that were almost erased by European colonizers is rising, especially among the young irrespective of the origins of the ethnicity to which they belong. Which is why a Lula would have much more appeal among the population of Brazil than a Bolsonaro.

Such a mood dovetails with both the experience of India as well as the US. In India and in the US, affirmative action has ensured that hitherto underprivileged sections of society are becoming more visible in the higher reaches of the governance system, just as they were in Brazil under President Lula da Silva. This commonality of experience will have the effect of drawing these countries together in a manner independent of the need to unite against authoritarian expansionism. The PRC has followed a policy since the 1980s of co-opting elites in target countries to ensure that their policies mesh with Beijing's requirements.[1] This has salience in a situation where the elites have a monopoly of effective authority, but falter when that authority is challenged by grassroots activism or by sections less advantaged than the ruling elites, as has been taking place in much of Africa and South America, as well as in Asia.

The US, given its close association with European colonial powers since Harry S. Truman's period—in the latter half of the 1940s and beyond—has also followed a policy aimed at co-opting the elites, which is still in operation in countries such as those belonging to the GCC. However, the force of US music, literature, education, movies and other 'soft power' attributes has ensured an affinity towards the US as a country and a people (as distinct from being merely a government) in segments of the community far more in number than the elite in several countries in Africa, Asia and South America. Although the PRC has sought to replicate this, such an effort has not succeeded

---

[1] David O. Shullman, 'Protect the Party: China's Growing Influence in the Developing World', Brookings, January 22, 2019, https://www.brookings.edu/articles/protect-the-party-chinas-growing-influence-in-the-developing-world/.

thus far.[2] In contrast, less owing to government intervention than through the tapestry of its cultural offerings, India has been more successful, especially in Southeast Asia and in Africa.

Should a similar dissemination of cultural expressions from India take place in South America, that continent too is likely to be receptive in a manner that it has not been to directed and well-funded efforts by Beijing to broaden the soft power reach of the PRC. The problem is that the penetration by PRC-linked entities of meta data sources within the population of countries has been growing at speed. As a consequence, the flow of such meta data into China through PRC-origin mobile telephone systems, online gaming, PRC-controlled apps and other means appears to have already outpaced the meta data reaching the US, the other superpower in this new contest. This has taken place despite the much longer head start that the latter had in the collection of meta data that is inter alia vital for continued improvements in Artificial Intelligence capabilities that could be of transformative importance in the hybrid war that is taking place between the two camps.

In the twenty-first century, any 'black and white' differentiation of society would be incorrect. The reason is that within the 'white' community itself, there is a growing acceptance of the inevitability (and to many the desirability) of a multiracial society. Hollywood movies are beginning to feature wealthy 'black' men and their (sometimes wealthy) 'white' girlfriends, and such portrayals are coming true within society increasingly. Interracial couples and children are becoming commonplace, except in locations where economic opportunities are few, so that migration from other parts

---

[2] George Gao, 'Why Is China So . . . Uncool?', *Foreign Policy*, March 8, 2017, https://foreignpolicy.com/2017/03/08/why-is-china-so-uncool-soft-power-beijing-censorship-generation-gap/.

of the country does not take place. The proportion of the white population subscribing to the Afrikaner South Africa model was low in 2016. But for Trump's reaching out to 'poor whites' (especially those that had been rendered jobless by shutdowns caused by relocation of production units to other countries), he would not have bested his Democratic Party challenger Hillary Clinton, who was herself unpopular with large sections of the electorate because of a perception that the Clintons had developed a sense of entitlement to the White House. During his 2017 presidency, Trump was so focused on ensuring tax breaks for the wealthy that he made it possible for the folksy Biden to take away enough of the white voters who had favoured Trump four years ago to defeat the sitting US president (Obama) with a substantial margin. Trump's racially tinged policies and rhetoric assisted Biden in mobilizing the 'non-white' vote to an unprecedented degree in 2020, a factor that proved crucial to his victory. Should the Democratic Party retain control of the House of Representatives and secure a majority in the Senate, the implementation of social welfare policies of the Biden-Harris administration is likely to ensure societal stability in the US in a manner that the more exclusivist approach adopted by President Trump was incapable of achieving.

Rule by the people (Demos) is definitely not in vogue in actual practice, even in several democracies, where money and connections count for far more than mere numbers. The US Congress is hardly representative of the people of the country, with most of its members having joined the higher reaches of society in terms of their wealth. This is particularly the case in the US Senate, where the average annual income of its 100 members comes up to millions of dollars. However, the US system provides for a separation of powers not just between the executive, the judiciary and the legislature, but between the media, civil society, industry, political parties and other elements that wield power individually without being under the control of other segments. In contrast, the Standing Committee of the CPC led by the general secretary exercises overriding authority over the other branches of the state through the monopoly of the party over governmental authority. The Mandate of Heaven[3] is assumed as a given by the CPC leadership and has been based since 1949 on popular pride in the ascent within the international space of the PRC during Mao's period in office.

To this was added in the 1980s the benefits of economic expansion and the consequent upward movement of average incomes. General Secretary Xi has brought out of the closet the 'Chinese Dream', first unveiled during the period in office of Hu Jintao. Essentially, this is the dream of once again emerging as the pivot of global geopolitics, thereby recapturing the status of the Middle Kingdom. Unlike any of his predecessors since Mao, General Secretary Xi has been transparent in his efforts at displacing the US as the primary power on the globe. Just as its numero uno status enabled the US to get substantial economic benefit, that status will do the same for China, according to Xi, especially if the RMB replaces the US dollar as the reserve currency of the world and global logistics and technology chains have Beijing as the hub rather than Washington. That, at least, is the plan.

---

[3] In the annals of Chinese history, there exists a political and philosophical notion known as the Mandate of Heaven. According to this concept, rulers are given legitimacy by their divine right to rule the universe. This idea arose during the Zhou dynasty, extending over nearly three centuries (1046–256 BCE). The prominence of this belief has had an enduring effect on Chinese politics and culture for years gone by.

While there were tailwinds during the era of Mao Zedong (1949–75), considerable headwind was created by the impact of his decision to enter the Korean War in 1950 on the attitudes of the 'non-aligned' world. The activism of Mao contrasted with the more sedate albeit eloquently expressed policies of Jawaharlal Nehru, and the ascendance of Mao over Nehru even in the 'non-aligned' group was cemented by the 1962 victory of the PRC over India in the October–November border war. Additional tailwind was created by the 1972 rapprochement between the US and China illustrated in the meeting between President Nixon and Chairman Mao. Soon after Deng Xiaoping took over as the paramount leader of China in 1978, the experience gained during the 1979 invasion of Vietnam propelled him away from Mao's propensity towards the use of force in the settlement of disputes with other countries. The Deng line of hiding the big stick while making it ever bigger assisted the PRC in convincing the rest of the world that its rise would have only benign consequences for them, an attitude that lasted until 2012, when Xi returned to Mao's policy of resort to force (or the threat thereof).

The principal protagonists in this era of Cold War 2.0, the PRC and the US, have each committed self-goals. An example was President Trump's decision to withdraw from the Trans-Pacific Partnership and the Iran nuclear deal. In both instances, Beijing stepped into the vacuum created by the US withdrawal, much as it is seeking to do (in conjunction with Pakistan and its proxies) in Afghanistan, now that President Biden has in 2021 repeated President Clinton's 1996 error of facilitating the takeover of that country by the Taliban.

Much has been said, especially in PRC media as well as in the media of countries allied to China such as the Russian Federation, of the 'chaos' in the US and India, although old ties have softened the media sallies against India in Russia to levels much below what they are with reference to the US. Certainly, both democracies exhibit signs that in China especially would be regarded as chaotic, punctuated with situations such as mobs attacking locations in the national capital, as it took place in Delhi and Washington not long ago. However, just as an individual who has been addicted to a substance for a long time develops higher levels of tolerance to the effects of a fresh dose of the narcotic, both the US and India have evolved systems that are able to bear the shocks from such events. In contrast, the system in the PRC necessitates a swift and crushing response to any and all such symptoms of unrest and dissatisfaction, so that a sustained spike in such events would have far greater effects on the governance system in Beijing than they would in Delhi or Washington. The safety valves created by a higher tolerance for even vigorous forms of dissent that the democracies possess, give them an inner political sustainability and societal stability that is lacking in an authoritarian state. The response of the Chinese state to the 1989 mass manifestation of dissent against existing authority in Tiananmen Square by Deng or the 1999 brutal crackdown on the Falun Gong by General Secretary Jiang Zemin after several thousand practitioners of that theology ringed the Zhongnanhai government quarter in Beijing was due to the higher degree of vulnerability of the system of governance established by Mao Zedong in 1949 in the PRC to such manifestations.

What this means in practice is that the level of mass civil unrest required to severely damage the PRC governance system would be much less than what would be required to start disintegration of the structure of democratic authorities. It is not accidental that the public discontent described as the Arab Spring had its success in countries that were authoritarian and left untouched those who either were not, or where the lives of the people were at a level satisfactory to them. More than a call for democracy, the 2011 Tahrir Square uprising against the dictator of Egypt Hosni Mubarak was a cry for more and cheaper bread. In the case of Communist China, it must be remembered that the standard of living of the people, despite being low during Mao's era, was an improvement over what it had been during the warlord era. At the same time, Chairman Mao kept rebellion at bay by appealing to the pride of the (Han) people through doubling the territory of the country and instilling a siege mentality. Not to mention snuffing out an expected future rebellion by launching the 1966 Great Proletarian Cultural Revolution, among the most disruptive movements ever seen in the long history of China. Given that the standard of living of the population in the PRC has risen substantially once the Deng reforms got under way in the 1980s, any slowdown of the rise in the standard of living (much less a reduction) would cause a weakening of the Mandate of Heaven so far as the acceptance by the population of the authority of the CPC is concerned. Which is why Xi has brought into use the Mao-era tools of creating a siege mentality and is seeking to generate pride in a steady expansion of PRC-controlled sea and land territory. The CPC General Secretary believes that this would act as compensation for a slowdown in the economy and a consequent deceleration in living standards caused by the fallout of Cold War 2.0.

Whether against the US in Korea or later in Vietnam, or against India, Mao never lost any of the wars that he fought, including the pre-1949 battles with the Japanese Army of occupation and the KMT. Should Xi find his country locked in an all-out battle with India in the Himalayan massif, and should the PLA be seen to lose to the Indian side, the effect on the CPC and on the general secretary in particular would be severe. This is a factor leading the US and Japan to come forward with offers to assist India, in the advent of another major kinetic contest with China. A combination of US assistance in intelligence and weaponry and that of Japan and Australia to ensure that the temperature rises for the PLA in other theatres could facilitate such a victory by the armed forces of the Republic of India. Given the secrecy with which government operates in India, it is difficult to tell if such preparations are under way for a war that seems likely to take place during the next few years, given the friskiness of the PLA vis-à-vis its Indian counterpart since the Xi era because of its linkage with GHQ Rawalpindi and the much bigger economic heft of the PRC. Just as Japan was internally portrayed as an inferior country in Tsarist Russia, so is India portrayed in the PRC. Which is why military defeat at the hands of India in the ongoing contest taking place in the Himalayan massif would impact the governance system in China much the way the defeat at Tsushima did in Tsarist Russia in 1905.

If anything, Taiwan is portrayed within the PRC by the CPC information apparatus in terms that are much more dismissive and contemptuous than is the case with India. That island country, which is a global tech hub, is regarded as an appendage that needs not to be cut loose like a diseased appendix but integrated into the PRC. Given the placing by Xi of the Chinese military as the centrepiece of strategy in China, expectations are high that such an integration will come about during Xi's tenure by force if the Taiwanese are tired to continue fighting for their freedom to being absorbed by a country much larger than their own and a system of governance that is in most particulars the opposite of their own. The effort has been and will continue to be to (a) persuade Taiwan that resistance is futile and therefore the sensible course is surrender; and (b) ensure through a demonstration of PLA capabilities that it would be folly for

Washington to come to the assistance of Taipei in the event of an armed conflict with Beijing. Neither condition seems close to being fulfilled. The Tsai government in Taiwan is building up its strike capability rather than cogitating on a surrender, while President Biden is as aware as the CIA and the Pentagon that the loss of Taiwan would render the US presence in the Indo-Pacific of little value to those countries refusing to take the side of the Sino-Russian alliance. Japan would go nuclear in terms of weapons capability, South Korea would be at the mercy of the North, especially if Pyongyang is allied to Beijing to force a unification on terms that humiliate its non-nuclear cousin to the south. The Philippines would switch from being a US to a PRC ally, as would other countries in the region. India would face relentless harassment if not kinetic attack from the Sino-Pakistan alliance, while the Middle East would move from Washington's to Beijing's tent. There is much at stake in any kinetic contest between Taiwan and China. Which is why it is unlikely that the US (or Japan) would remain uninvolved in the event of a cross-straits war. Should China be bested in an attempt to take over Taiwan, the effects on the governance system established by the CPC would be devastating. As would be the consequence of a military defeat at the hands of India in a replay in reverse of the 1962 Sino-Indian war. Which is why ensuring the defence of Taiwan and India is a much greater need for US and Atlanticist interests in general than getting involved in a quagmire over Ukraine that merely nudges ever closer the already existing Sino-Russian partnership.

11

Reason and Not Emotion
Needs to Drive Policy

The first half of the twentieth century witnessed two World Wars. The relationship between the US and the USSR deteriorated soon after their alliance during the conflict with Germany during what is commonly termed as World War II ended with the close of that war in 1945. A year earlier, the United Nations Organization was conceived by the Allied powers to prevent conflict, at least between the major powers. The USSR joined the US and the UK at the High Table, represented by their becoming permanent members of the UN Security Council, the body tasked with keeping the peace. During the discussions which took place regarding the setting up of the UN, UK Prime Minister Churchill succeeded in keeping India out of the privileged club of the UNSC Permanent Members (P-5). This was despite the reality of over two million volunteers from India being part of the Allied armies that finally overcame both Germany and its partner in the Axis, Japan. Churchill was candid in his admission that he did not believe that those of an ethnicity different from that of the European people had a place in any table at all, whether high or low. Their role was, in his view, to remain in the kitchen carrying out the orders of their betters. While excluding India, Churchill ensured that France was included in the Big Five, despite that country having been under the occupation of German forces for much of the war. Roosevelt may not have succeeded in persuading Churchill to include India, but he was successful in adding (then KMT-ruled) China to the club. These discussions mostly took place in 1944, and the world is now in the third decade of the twenty-first century, while the UNSC remains as it was when first conceived. India may soon be the third largest economy in the world and the country with the largest population, but the chances of it being accepted as a permanent member of the UNSC are close to nil. Overall, the UN, and the UNSC, provided a forum for conversations that resulted in the avoidance of any direct conflict between the two superpowers of the era, the USSR and the US, although proxy wars were plentiful. At least in this, the UN may be characterized as a success.

During Cold War 1.0 between the USSR and the US, the leaders of the former in particular were wary of getting into a direct conflict with the US in the manner that the PRC under Mao Zedong had during the 1950–53 Korean War. During the 1962 Cuban Missile Crisis, it was CPSU General Secretary Khrushchev who blinked and not President Kennedy, a factor that was likely to have played a role in his ouster by the Politburo two years later. Even during the proxy war with the US occasioned by the Soviet invasion of Afghanistan, because Pakistan had been a treaty ally of the US, the Soviet leadership held back from doing what was militarily necessary in order to avoid defeat in Afghanistan, which was to attack the bases within Pakistan that trained, equipped and in other ways facilitated the Mujahideen battling against Soviet forces and their Afghan allies. The avoidance of direct conflict between any of the members of the UNSC P-5 entered uncharted territory in 2014, when widespread and sometimes violent street protests in Ukraine, which seemed as much orchestrated as they were spontaneous, succeeded in driving out the country's elected Russian-speaking head of state, Viktor Yanukovych, not just from power but from the country itself. Given his reading of the lessons gleaned from the experience of the Kremlin with the Atlanticist powers from the 1960s onwards, President Putin came to the conclusion that the ouster of Yanukovych was the first stage in a NATO operation designed to pit Ukraine kinetically against the Russian Federation. This resulted in the Russian annexation of Crimea as well as the creation of the Donetsk and Lugansk republics through the instrumentality of the Russian military during the same year as the Yanukovych ouster. From that time onwards, NATO led by the US and the Russian Federation have entered upon a course that is already taking on the characteristics of a direct conflict between the two entities, for the first time ever. The proxy war being waged by NATO against Russia on the territory of Ukraine has had the effect of giving oxygen to PRC efforts at expanding its control over land, sea, air and now space in various locations. Ukraine is as important to the security of the Russian Federation as Taiwan is to the security of Japan, a keystone partner of the US. As one of the four Great Powers of the age (together with the US, China and India), reason would dictate that Russia ought to have its core security interests remain unaffected by formations that are clearly hostile to the country—a description that 2022 has shown fits NATO fairly well. The manner of response of the US and the UK in particular (if we leave aside the Baltic states and Poland, which have history as a reason for a similar attitude) to the war launched by Russia in Ukraine on 24 February 2022 can only be described as being driven by undiluted emotion.

There have been episodes in democracies where the former head of state lands up in prison at the hands of his or her predecessor soon after demitting office. South Korea was an example, although such a dynamic appears not to be operational in the latest change in the official occupant of the Blue House in Seoul. In an authoritarian state, removal from high office often entails severe costs not just in terms of wealth and authority but often even freedom itself for the former high dignitary and those in what gets termed as his or her coterie. Prevailing over the Ukrainian leadership since Russia's launch of a Special Military Operation (aka war) against Ukraine is almost certainly an existential issue for President Putin. Should Moscow lose the ongoing contest with Kiev (which in changing forms has been going on since 2014), Putin and most likely his close family and friends would be fortunate were they to escape with their savings and their freedom. The wisdom of putting an individual with a briefcase containing nuclear codes close by his side may not entirely be prudent. The usual consequences for a loss of power by a politician in most democracies is not what they potentially are for those heading an authoritarian regime, especially in a country that has throughout its history known only such governments.

Delight in the capitals of NATO member states at reports of presumed setbacks for the Russian military against the Ukrainian resistance ignore the fact that the weaker Putin's kinetic hand gets, the bigger his incentive to resort to some of the deadlier weapons that the Russian Federation possesses in substantial quantities. Technology has enabled the development of 'tactical nuclear weapons' that have a limited impact, and which are capable of being used in battlefield conditions. The use of a nuclear weapon in a combat is never tactical'. It is invariably a strategic choice. And confronted with a choice between ignominy on the field of war or the use of nuclear weapons to stun into submission Ukrainian forces may result in the latter choice being adopted by the Kremlin.

Despite reports mostly in Atlanticist media about the civilian toll of Russian military strikes in Ukrainian territory, the fact remains that even at the time of writing this work in late 2022, the battleground has largely remained confined to those parts of the country that have a preponderant majority of citizens who are 'Russian-speaking' (rather than 'Ukrainian-speaking', a distinction that is slender in depth, the two languages being if not twins then at least first cousins to each other). Such a concentration of attention indicates that a key strategic purpose of the 'Special Military Operation' is to secure the Donbass and Lugansk territories from Kiev in a manner similar to what took place in Crimea in 2014. Since February–March 2022, there have been voices that said that the wisest course for President Volodymyr Zelenskyy of Ukraine would include going by the example of Georgia and accept in practice the loss of the territories that were in control of the new 'republics' before the latest war began on 24 February 2022. Instead, he opted for a maximalist policy of seeking to regain the territories lost to the Russian Federation since 2014, including Crimea. In the process, Ukraine has been devastated and it is unlikely that the close of this conflict would result in only the loss of territory that would have been possible had the Ukrainian leader accepted the status quo rather than preparing to alter it to the status quo ante before the 2014 ouster of Yanukovych.

There is logic behind the efforts of the US to weaken Russia and those of the PRC to do the same to India. Where the EU is concerned, Russia is the only country that has the potential to displace the US as the primary partner from outside that grouping. Where Asia is concerned, India is the only country that has the potential to displace China as the lead power within the continent. A verdict needs to be given on the benefits or otherwise of the EU following the US and the UK substantively and through kinetic means backing the maximalist position of the Ukrainian leadership in the matter of the territory lost to pro-Moscow entities since 2014. Blocking off the flow of resources and shutting the doors of conciliation and cooperation with a country that has the largest Gross National Resources (GNR) in the world, besides possibly the world's deadliest nuclear arsenal, appears to be more the result of emotion than of reason where the interests of the EU are concerned. Ukraine is admittedly rich in foodgrain and in oil and gas, as is Russia or the US. However, the EU countries are not. Some economies would be severely impacted were they to cut themselves off from access to raw materials from the Russian Federation. Neither the US nor the GCC, nor both together, are able to match the unique economic and logistical advantages of supply from Russia. In such a context, Germany not taking advantage of the completed Nord Stream II pipeline but in effect rendering the pipeline ineffective appears to be an exercise in self-harm on a potentially disastrous scale.

During the 1962 Cuban Missile Crisis, there were no usable 'tactical' nuclear weapons, only much larger ones that needed to be launched from locations far from the target zone. In the third decade of the twenty-first century, nuclear warheads that are much smaller in size and effect than even those used in Hiroshima and Nagasaki in 1945 are in the armoury of the Russian Federation. An organization that has Article 5, promising a kinetic response by all member states to an attack on any member, needed to be far more parsimonious in admitting new members (and thereby taking on greater potential commitments) than has been witnessed in NATO since the collapse of the USSR in the closing days of 1991. The use of a nuclear weapon on a NATO member state that is very vulnerable to a Russian land attack, such as on the Baltic states, would present Washington and Brussels with the problem of whether or not to risk an expanded nuclear exchange with the Russian Federation by using 'tactical' nuclear weapons on Russian troops or territory should President Putin up the ante significantly by attacking a Baltic country with nuclear weapons. Or launch a direct conventional war on the Russian Federation, should that country's military invade a Baltic country through the utilization of conventional weaponry.

What would NATO's response be if Moscow were to follow the example of Washington in 1945 and use nuclear weapons on Ukrainian forces to compel that country to sue for peace on the terms insisted from the start by Putin, namely loss of the Russian-speaking areas and the demilitarization and neutralization of the rest of Ukraine? What is taking place in that unfortunate country appears to be a situation that involves pushing a nuclear-armed adversary into a corner such that its leadership believes that it has less and less to lose should it raise the stakes in battle exponentially. Should such an outcome come about, the course being pursued by NATO in Ukraine may in hindsight be seen as having had a far bigger cost to it than any benefit that was possible, had the policy worked by ensuring the defeat of Russia by Ukraine. It is such a risk that is being faced by the international community today, even as the proxy war between NATO and the Russian Federation that is presently being fought on the territory of Ukraine, even if it somehow manages to avoid a direct conflict between the two entities, has devastated large portions of the global economy and caused immense misery to populations that are wholly outside the countries that form NATO.

Epilogue
The Bonfire of the Optimists

Fifty years ago, Prime Minister Indira Gandhi decided to release the 93,000 Pakistan Army prisoners of war captured by Indian and Mukti Bahini forces during the 1971 Bangladesh War. Although several thousand of them had identifiably committed acts of murder, rape and plunder, none was subjected to trial. Their genocidal actions were in effect pardoned by the Government of India. Far from engendering a mood of conciliation within the Pakistan Army, the gesture shown by India was quickly forgotten and replaced with feelings of vengeance that within a dozen years manifested themselves in causing the flames of violence and insurgency to burn in Punjab and Kashmir. By the middle of the 1980s, activities began in Kashmir that culminated in a violent insurgency, embers of which continue to simmer even today. If Nehru fashioned the foreign policy of India to fit the kind of world he wished to see rather than the world as it was, his successors came up with policy towards Pakistan and the other country that had taken as its own large tracts of Kashmir, China, grounded in their belief in the adage, 'One good turn deserves (and so would result in) another.'

Over and over again, turning the other cheek resulted only in that too getting slapped, and yet the action continued to be repeated in a show of almost irrational optimism as the other side responded to concessions not by seeking more but by offering its own. If we were to substitute India and Pakistan with the US and China, events have made clear that initiatives taken by Washington to satiate Islamabad have yielded negligible returns to the bigger country. Pakistan was supposed to help ensure that the Taliban kept its promise of change in 2021, rather than revert back to what it had been in 2001. As in the 1980s in the war within Afghanistan against the USSR, in the 1990s and inexplicably after the expulsion of the Taliban in 2001 as well, much of the war on the terror elements that had been, and remained, an essential part of the toolkit of GHQ Rawalpindi was outsourced by the US to Pakistan, a state that even then was far more under the influence of Beijing rather than Washington.

The inevitable resurgence of the Taliban followed on the heels of US and allied policy of propitiating Pakistan and by implication its proxies, including that which NATO was battling with, the Taliban. The *tertius gaudens*, the gainer in the middle, has been Communist China, which since its founding in 1949 has sought to divert US and allied attention away from itself, in the way that happened after 9/11 or once Russian troops invaded Ukraine on 24 February 2022. Even after the fall of the USSR in 1991, the Clinton administration welcomed China into the WTO and opened the store to US technology and investment in a hitherto unprecedented manner. Rather than mellow into a social democracy, as the China experts clustered around the White House calculated, the PRC has become more autocratic and more menacing, especially to its immediate neighbours.

Whether it be the provision of covert assistance to PRC-linked groups in Myanmar, Thailand or India that are seeking to extinguish the control of the central authority in territories saturated by such groups. A more direct method followed by the CPC leadership has been through takeovers of offshore space internationally accepted as belonging to Vietnam and the Philippines, among other target states. By now, the PRC has emerged in plain view as a predatory power that wherever feasible abandons the pretence of restraint in fulfilling ever-expanding territorial and other control objectives of the CPC leadership.

Just as 9/11 was, the Ukraine conflict has come as a boon to the PRC, which is now being courted rather than looked askance at by countries facing the North Atlantic. Once again, as during Cold War 1.0 between the US and the USSR, even in this era of Cold War 2.0 between China and the US principally, the invasion of Ukraine by Russian forces has led to a shift in resources and attention by the western powers from the Indo-Pacific back to the Atlantic, from Asia back to Europe, from China to Russia. There is something about the chemistry of policymaking within democracies that generates an often-irrational faith in the mutually—repeat, mutually—beneficial effects of one-sided concessions. The change is that the public in such countries is increasingly drawing conclusions about the overall situation that are at odds with the continuation of efforts at appeasement of obvious foes. Whether it be appeasing the Wahhabi component of the Sino-Wahhabi alliance by abandoning Afghanistan to an unreformed Taliban, or by refusing to funnel arms to Taiwan or in the profusion and favourable terms shown to Ukraine, top policymakers leading the charge of the appeasement brigade are seeing their popularity shrink. The world is witnessing a bonfire of the optimists that may result in the lessons of the 1930s in Europe being factored in rather than ignored in the Asia of the 2020s.

In twentieth-century terms, we are now in 1937. The only way that a rerun of 1939–45 can be avoided is for the major democracies, especially the two great powers among them, India and the US, to acknowledge this, and to fashion policies that are grounded not in the hopes and illusions of the past, but on the rock of present-day reality.